To my darling Leon!

I promise I won't fall asleep for your first Chinese meal!

Happy Christmas 1982.

love & kisses

Eugénie

x x x x x x x x x x

6 -
80

D1293956

CHINESE

DELIGHTS

CHINESE

by Lisa Kinsman with photographs by Christine Hanscomb

DELIGHTS

Book Club Associates, London

CHINESE DELIGHTS
This edition published 1982 by
Book Club Associates by arrangement with
Jill Norman & Hobhouse Ltd
90 Great Russell Street
London WC1B 3PY

Christine Hanscomb's photographs and portions of Lisa
Kisman's text appeared in the Habitat *Cook's Diary*,
1981, and are reproduced by permission of Conran
Designs Ltd.

Typeset by V & M Graphics Ltd, Aylesbury, Bucks
Printed and bound in Hong Kong by
Everbest Printing Company Limited

CONTENTS

Introduction   6
Regional Cooking   11
Utensils   13
Recipes:
  Sesame Chicken   16*
  Szechuan Green Beans   18
  Roast Beggar Chicken   20
  Stir-fried Prawns with spring onions   22*
  Sliced Pork with Wooden Ears   24
  Drunken Fish   26
  Stir-fried Boiled Rice   27
  Lion's Head   28*
  Smoked Quail   30
  Chinese Cabbage   31
  Jung   32*
  Wun-Tun Soup with Watercress   34
  Braised Leg of Pork   36*
  Chicken in Plum Sauce   38
  Lemon Beef Soup   40*
  Yam Noodles   42
  Stir-fried Scallops   44
  Bean Paste Chicken with Green Peppers   46
  Spring Rolls   48
  Beef and Green Peppers with Fried Noodles   50
  Fried Rice   52
  Peking Duck   54
  Fried Sweet and Sour Wun-Tun   56
  Toffee Apples and Bananas   58
  Stir-fried Mangetout Peas and Chinese Sausage   60
  Boiled Noodles   62

Beef with Black Soy Beans   64
Chicken with Pickled Vegetables   66
Deep-fried Spicy Rolls   68
Lin-Go   70
Stir-fried Chicken with Broad Beans   72
My Cake   74*
Spring Onion Savoury   76
Stir-fried Lamb with Green Peppers and Pancakes   78
Steamed Trout or Sea Bass   80
Paper Parcels   82
Stuffed Fillet of Sole   84
Cantonese Pork Fillet   86*
Transparent Noodles with Dried Shrimps   88
Stir-fried Prawns with Ginger   90
Steamed Grey Mullet with Lemon   92
Steamed Fresh Scallops   94
Chicken with Leeks   96
Chicken with Celery   98
Green and White Chicken Soup   100
Spinach Parcel Soup   102
Smoked Halibut   104
Spare Ribs   106*
Stuffed Aubergines   108*
Chilled Snow Ears with Kiwi Fruit   110
Ingredients   112
Techniques   123
Cooking Methods   124
Index   127

* Dishes which can be prepared in advance or need little last-minute attention.

INTRODUCTION

Since Chinese food is now very popular, with a wide choice of restaurants offering different regional cuisines, more and more people are tempted to cook some of the dishes at home. This book is designed to help them create in their own kitchens something as nearly authentic, but at the same time practical, as possible. Once the basic techniques have been mastered, recipes can be expanded and altered to suit individual tastes, or even invented from scratch. This is not just the prerogative of the expert – in fact experimentation and improvisation are essential in Chinese cooking, which is largely intuitive.

The essence of successful Chinese cooking lies in the careful preparation of the ingredients in advance. Although this seems to demand a lot of time and effort, it is more than justified by the results. It is important to work steadily and methodically during the actual cooking in order to achieve a perfect combination of colour, texture and flavour. Also, I cannot overstress the importance of presentation. The food must look good as well as tasting good, and should always do justice to the effort that went into its production.

By way of introduction, I would like to give some idea of the way in which Chinese people eat, starting with the most elaborate meals. I remember from my childhood in Hong Kong, that whenever there was a big social occasion it was always celebrated with a banquet – sometimes for as many as a thousand people. The banquet, which could run to fifteen courses, would begin with at least four light and tasty dishes to arouse the appetite, followed by an extravagant soup such as shark's fin or dried abalone. After that would come at least one course each of meat, poultry, fish and game, cooked in different ways. On some occasions a whole roast suckling pig would be served. Then there might be another, simpler, soup and one or two more meat or vegetable dishes after that. Should all this not be enough, a fried rice and noodles course would be served in order to satisfy any still-hungry guests. Noodle dishes, incidentally, are considered propitious for long life.

Finally, dessert. This would not have the status of a full-blown course, rather it would be a formality, to signify the end of the meal. Occasionally it could be a true delicacy, such as silver ears (a white tree fungus, steamed in honey with a little liquid) or a light, creamy soup of lotus seeds or almonds. One might be expected to fast all day in anticipation of such a feast but when it came, protocol demanded that one should not eat heartily but only sample each dish, even though the host is judged on the quality and quantity of the food served.

Normal everyday eating is, of course, quite a different affair. For a family of five or six persons, a meal would usually consist of four to five dishes, eaten with plain boiled rice, favoured by the southern Chinese, or steamed wheat bread in the north. The rice or bread serves not only as ballast, but also to neutralise the taste of each dish and to clean the palate. Thus one takes a little of each dish at a time, in between a mouthful of rice or bread.

Food also plays a large part in the religious festivals which, together with the family, are the mainstays of the Chinese way of life. The principal religion is Buddhism, with many gods to appease and ancient customs surviving to the present day. There are separate festivals to pay homage to each god in turn, and these always involve a special peace-offering of food. But perhaps the most important tradition is the ceremony of paying respect to one's ancestors by visiting the graveside with the whole family, bringing offerings of cooked food. I remember that, before one of these occasions, my mother would make a particular family speciality consisting of ground rice dough, pressed into a round decorative mould and filled with shredded, seasoned vegetables or crushed soya-bean paste. This would be steamed and given as a gift to the relatives and close friends after the ceremony. To be sure of obtaining the best quality flour for these cakes my mother would even take the trouble of grinding a huge quantity of rice with a grinder, not unlike a mechanical pestle and mortar but large enough to need two people to operate the foot pedal. So elaborate were the preparations for this kind of occasion that the help of relatives or friends would be needed, and it would become a social occasion in itself.

Among the many festivals there is one celebrated in the spring which is especially associated with the dish 'Jung' (*page* 32). According to legend, there was, about three thousand years ago, an important politician and poet in the Imperial Court who was falsely accused by rivals of populist sympathies. In despair he drowned himself. His friends and followers searched in vain for his body, and then invented a special food – Jung – which they threw into the sea so that the fishes should eat it rather than their friend. Ever since, Jung has been a symbolic peace-offering associated with the spring. and is eaten by the Chinese instead of being wasted on the fish. It is made of glutinous rice combined with well-flavoured meat, water chestnuts, Chinese mushrooms and a little spice, and wrapped in bamboo leaves. In China the little parcels are tied up with dried reeds, with a long end left loose, so that eight to ten of the reeds can be plaited together; once cooked, the separate collections of parcels can be hung from a long pole fixed high over the kitchen or storeroom. This not only keeps the food fresh, but looks very decorative.

I remember with particular affection another festival, which is a favourite among children, called the Moon Festival. This is to pay homage to the moon goddess, and it falls in the middle of August. It is celebrated with the special 'moon cake' which is made from crushed lotus-seed paste, with one or two duck egg yolks (symbolising the moon), contained in a light, pretty patterned casing. It is very rich and sweet and one can eat only small slivers at a time. Since the moon is brightest at this time of year it is perfect for the ceremony in the evening. The children run around with lanterns of different animal shapes, made from coloured tissue paper wrapped round bamboo frames, with a lighted candle inside. It is hard to imagine a prettier sight.

The most important celebration of all is the Chinese New Year, which falls any time between the end of January and the middle of February (the calendar months in China are quite different from those in the west). Most families start their preparations for it by buying lots of delicacies such as Chinese dried mushrooms, abalone, shark's fin, silver ears, bird's nests, cured sausages, duck, and a large selection of dried vegetables – anything for a special treat.

It is always a great pleasure to entertain and serve relatives and friends with elaborate dishes. For instance there is the steamed pudding, 'Lin-Go' (see page 70), made with natural brown sugar and glutinous rice flour, very sweet to taste, somewhat similar to the British Christmas pudding but not as rich. Each one weighs at least a few pounds, depending on the size of the steamer one has, and can be kept fresh for at least two weeks. It is sliced into small pieces and fried until the surface is golden brown, and then it is served. Conscientious Buddhists eat only vegetarian food for the first three days of the New Year. In fact, devout Buddhists have always been strict vegetarians, but since there are hundreds of interesting vegetables, fresh, dried or pickled, dried tree fungi and plentiful varieties of soya bean curds, this is no hardship.

Most of the dishes in this book are calculated to serve approximately four to six people, in an arrangement of at least four separate dishes (of meat, fish, poultry or game) together with some kind of leaf or root vegetable and, of course, rice, noodles or steamed bread, perhaps also accompanied by a little bowl of clear, light soup. When planning for a dinner party you might wish to restrict the number of dishes (especially if you are a beginner) in order to reduce the work. This is perfectly reasonable provided you increase the quantity of all ingredients in the dishes you cook as well as the time allowed for cooking.

In most recipes some sugar is added to bring out the flavour of the ingredients. Although the amount I have indicated is my personal preference, it can be reduced to suit individual taste or dietetic needs.

It is a good idea to separate the preparation and the cooking when planning a meal. All cleaning, slicing or chopping of meat and vegetables should be carried out beforehand and prepared foods put into separate bowls and covered with cling-film to keep them fresh. I always think that if you have to start cooking the meal immediately after hours of preparation you may feel overworked and tired and not do justice to the actual cooking – still less the eating!

Before starting to cook make sure that all the seasonings such as soy sauce, salt and pepper, sugar, cooking oil, 'wet' cornflour (cornflour ready-mixed with cold water) are ready to hand by the cooker. Any of these may be needed at any time during the cooking process and the last thing you want is to have to go looking in cupboards or mixing up cornflour and water at a crucial stage of the operation. I would also suggest placing the ingredients for each dish in separate groups, so as to avoid confusion when cooking at speed. For an informal dinner party, all the dishes should be served together. But as it is impossible to cook them all simultaneously, the waiting dishes should be kept in a warm oven for a few minutes. The oven should be pre-heated, and the heat then switched off in order not to spoil the food. I also believe that part of the menu should be made up of dishes that can be cooked in advance and simply re-heated before serving, for example some stewed or braised food served together with last minute stir-fry or steamed dishes.

I must admit that the first attempts will not be easy. Most difficult is the adjustment of the heat and the timing (especially with the stir-fry method), even when all the preparation can be done in advance. For this reason, I have tried to stick to the simplest and easiest methods of producing day-to-day food. As the recipes I selected for this book are from various regions and styles of cooking, I have tried on the following pages to explain their origins and how they would be used in the daily Chinese menu.

Most Chinese people like to start the day with something hot and substantial to line the stomach, the equivalent, I suppose, of English bacon and eggs. Usually this would be congee, which is a kind of rice porridge cooked with a lot more water than rice, and simmered for about an hour until it becomes thick and bland. It is eaten plain, accompanied either with something salty, such as salted duck egg or salted fish, or some sort of cold, jellied meat or fish, creating the interesting contrast of very hot porridge and very cold savoury. Or else it is eaten with some very fine sliced meat, served with chopped spring onion, very finely shredded ginger root and coriander (Chinese parsley). Another popular breakfast is the soup/noodles dish. This is made with plenty of good stock and served with noodles, finely sliced meat and fresh herbs. It is all very unlike a European breakfast.

Most families will have a 'proper' cooked meal in the middle of the day as well as in the evening. Perhaps the food is slightly simpler and more economical at lunchtime, but for an average family it would certainly consist of four dishes as well as soup, which is served all through the meal. Soup is very popular with most Chinese people; it is always prepared with real meat or fish stock with various kinds of fresh leaf or root vegetables and is consumed in the same way as Europeans take wine or water with meals. It is also a very good way of making use of all ingredients without waste. For example if fillet of chicken or pork is needed for stir-fried dishes, the bones would be used for the soup.

There are also the famous tea-house lunches, called Dim Sum (meaning 'touch of heart'). This special type of food is for more informal and casual eating than the proper meal. It consists mainly of a very large selection of small, bite-sized pieces of steamed or fried dumpling, filled with delicious chopped prawn or meat, mostly steamed in bamboo steamers. In the proper 'Dim Sum' restaurants there will be many waiters or waitresses carrying several stacks of the bamboo steamers on a large tray or trolley, circulating among the tables and giving them out as requested. Food can be kept very hot in this kind of steamer. Sometimes there can be more than thirty varieties, including sweet ones, to choose from, and the lunch can be as leisurely and lengthy as one desires. At the end of the meal your bill is calculated by the number of empty baskets. This kind of meal can be eaten between 11 am and 5 pm every day of the week; when eaten late in the afternoon it is treated as the equivalent of an English tea.

The average Chinese family, even one with small children, likes to eat at least one meal a day together. Since this is usually the evening meal, taken between 6 and 7 pm, often the adults want a light supper by 11 pm and many restaurants cater for this special eating hour. The food may be not unlike that served for breakfast, but the popular restaurant is the one which serves only 'Wun-Tin-Mein', which are the little parcels filled with fresh shrimps and served with freshly made noodles in a good stock, sometimes with a plate of seasonal green vegetables, lightly blanched and seasoned with soy sauce.

REGIONAL COOKING

I am more than delighted that at last proper Chinese cooking is becoming widely appreciated in Europe. It has become recognised and classed with the best of French or Italian cuisine, even though until the last decade or so, only a poor substitute was available to Europeans. Until quite recently, for most expatriate Chinese, there were only a few restaurants serving authentic food, principally from southern China. But in recent years many more restaurants have opened, serving true Chinese food in pleasantly designed surroundings, paying much more attention to serving the food correctly and elegantly and often with many new or improvised dishes.

More and more Chinese people are making their homes all over the world and of course the cooking travels with them, starting new trends in eating. The two most popular cuisines, outside China or the Far East, must certainly be the Peking (northern school) and the Cantonese (southern school).

More recently restaurants have emerged which follow the Shanghai (eastern school) and Szechuan (western school) completing the four principal regional schools. If I dare to generalise, I feel that expatriate Chinese seem to prefer Cantonese and Shanghai cooking; the Pekingese and the Cantonese are most popular with the English: and Szechuan food is definitely most popular amongst the Americans. Although all these schools of cooking have something in common and have been influenced by each other through many centuries, they still remain quite distinct.

Cantonese or Southern Chinese Cooking

This is the region along the south-east coast of China, which has a milder climate than the northern region. It enables the farmers to produce many types of leaf and root vegetables, such as Choy-Sum, snow peas (mangetout), Chinese radish, Chinese okra (silk melon), etc, together with meat from a wide selection of farm animals.

There is also a vast quantity of fresh seafood available. This abundance is responsible for the very simple and fresh style of cooking, with light but perfect seasoning, largely stir-fried and steamed to bring out the natural taste of all the ingredients. The seafood is given the minimum amount of cooking in order not to spoil the delicate texture and taste and is generally eaten with boiled rice. Typical examples can be seen in the recipes for Steamed Trout (*page* 80) and Fresh Steamed Scallops (*page* 94).

Shanghai

Shanghai has always been considered to be the most important culinary centre of China. It was the first major seaport open to the west many centuries ago, where traders from all over China and the world gathered, and this had a great influence on the food. It was the most affluent society in China. In general, cooking oil is used a little more lavishly in Shanghai than in the rest of China; the dishes are richer and eaten with steamed bread instead of rice. The famous Un-sin Poy, meaning 'Silver Thread Bread', is by far the best to eat and is much lighter than the bread eaten in the north. They are also famous for their noodle dishes which are distinct from the south in their use of plain instead of egg noodles. Another speciality of the area is steamed and fried dumplings, eaten with vinegar; I know this sounds peculiar, but the vinegar does in fact enhance the taste. Well-known dishes include Lion's Head (*page* 28), and Chicken with Pickled Vegetables (*page* 66).

Szechuan

This kind of cooking comes from the western part of China, where the climate is extremely humid and because of this, chilli-flavoured dishes are common. The Chinese believe that the hot spice counteracts the effect of dampness and improves the appetite. People living in this area can often eat a whole chilli without flinching.

This influence has spread throughout China and a little dish of chilli sauce is always served on the table, as most Chinese like an added hot taste to their food. Garlic and ginger are also frequently used to flavour dishes and are included in most of the pickled and preserved vegetables. A typical dish is Szechuan Green Beans (*page* 18).

Peking and North China

In this region the climate is considerably colder. There are fewer fresh green vegetables, especially during the winter season and the gap is filled with many kinds of pickled or preserved varieties. The most important and typical vegetable is the Chinese cabbage (sometimes called Chinese leaves) which can be kept for weeks if stored correctly by hanging on a hook in an airy place.

Many sheep are kept in the north and consequently there are many dishes based on mutton and lamb. For this reason the northern food tends to taste a bit stronger and includes many slow-simmered dishes. In the past the cooking stove was very close to the sleeping quarters because slow cooking generates heat and kept people warm in the cold weather. The starch component of the meals is usually steamed bread made with wheat flour and the sauces are more copious, to provide juice to dip the bread in. The best examples of this cuisine are Braised Leg of Pork (*page* 36), Peking Duck (*page* 54) and Stir-Fried Lamb with Green Peppers (*page* 78).

UTENSILS

The Wok

The wok is a large steel frying-pan with sloping sides and a rounded bottom, which makes it easy to cook even a large quantity of food quickly and efficiently without spilling any of it over the side. It is especially useful for stir-fried dishes but is equally useful for steaming with the lid on, deep-frying, and boiling. I believe it is an advantage to cook on gas rather than on electricity, as you have far better and faster control over the heat supply. Occasionally, gas can be a little unpredictable, particularly if you are using it at a time when most of the local population is cooking their evening meal and the pressure drops, but you can easily adjust the cooking time.

If a wok is not available an ordinary large skillet or a frying-pan can be used as a substitute. On the other hand, if you are successful with your wok, I do feel it is justifiable to invest in a second one. It saves a lot of washing-up time and trouble when cooking for an elaborate dinner party which involves many different dishes.

Seasoning the Wok

Traditional woks are available either in stainless or mild steel. Apart from washing after use, the stainless-steel one needs no special attention. However, the mild steel one usually has a sticky protective coating when new, which must first be removed with hot water and washing-up liquid, or a non-scouring cream cleaner. *Never* use an abrasive scourer, as to do so is to invite rust.

It is only necessary to season a new wok once. When the surface has been freed of its sticky coating the wok should be seasoned, wiped dry and then heated over a high temperature. When it is hot, put in four tablespoons (60 ml) corn oil, (it will smoke a little). Turn off the heat, put in 2–3 slices of fresh ginger and 2 cloves of crushed garlic, making sure the oil reaches all parts of the surface, by swishing it round. Do this repeatedly for a few minutes, then remove both ginger and garlic and most of the oil, leaving just enough to rub in all over the interior of the work, with kitchen paper. The wok will now have a very thin coat of oil for protection against rust. Each time the wok has been used and cleaned it is important to oil it.

Wok Ring

This is a circular steel ring with a few holes for ventilation, designed to ensure that the wok will rest safely on the burner of the cooker. At least two sizes can be purchased in most Chinese grocery stores. It is best to choose the shallowest ring, which enables the wok to get closest to the flame. Once you have mastered the art of cooking with a wok, it is more flexible to cook stir-fried dishes without a ring. (Do be careful, however, to cook with extra care at first to prevent food from burning). When steaming, deep-frying or boiling, it is absolutely essential to use the ring to prevent accidents, especially if there are children or animals about.

Steaming Basket and Steaming Rack

The steaming basket is a traditional round bamboo steamer with an open-weave base. They come in large and small sizes and can be stacked in tiers, enabling several different dishes to be steamed together. As the baskets are very decorative, food is not normally transferred after steaming but served in the containers directly on the table. This method of cooking is largely used in the preparation of 'Dim Sum' savoury snacks, usually eaten for lunch. A whole fish or pieces of meat can be cooked in a little liquid on a plate placed in a steaming basket. If a bamboo steamer is not available, you can substitute a steaming rack, which is a small circular metal rack, with three little feet resting in the centre of the wok, or dipping on to the sides. In both cases, a wok lid or a bamboo lid must be used in order to retain the steam.

Sand Pot

This is a perfect utensil for slow cooking – braising stew or making soup. It is made of coarse earthenware with a dark brown glazed interior (a perfect contrast in colour) and can be seen on pages 37 and 97. It is not unlike the earthenware casserole in most European countries and the only difference is that it is used on top of the stove and not in the oven. It is necessary to soak all sand pots in cold water for at least 24 hours before using for the first time. This treatment will prevent cracking. Please also remember never to cook on too high a temperature, as only a low heat is required anyway. An asbestos mat or boiling ring can be used.

Cleaver

If you own a cleaver with a very sharp edge, together with a good solid chopping-board, you have already won half the battle on mastering the arts and techniques of Chinese cooking.

There are several different sizes of cleaver to choose from, and the choice depends totally on individual preference. Personally, I prefer to use a smaller size cleaver, with a thin blade for slicing in order to achieve the finest results and a larger and heavier one for chopping through meat with bone. Once the food has been cut, a good way of removing it from the chopping-board is to slide the flat blade underneath, and transport the prepared food to a bowl. Cleavers can be sharpened on an oil-stone or with a steel. They should be lightly oiled after use and kept in a dry place. Often crushed ingredients, such as garlic or ginger, are required and this can be easily done by hitting the piece of whatever you need with the flat side of the cleaver or by placing the cleaver on top and banging it with your fist. Equally, it is useful to use the end of the handle to crush herbs or spices.

Scoop

This implement is similar to a soup ladle, only with a slightly larger bowl and it is quite a versatile tool. For example it can be used during stir-frying and also for scooping the food out of the wok into the serving dish very quickly to keep it as hot as possible.

Spatula or Wok-Stirrer

This looks like a metal spade with a long handle, available in different sizes. It is also commonly used in stir-frying, enabling you to turn over all the ingredients as well as scrape the bottom of the wok. If you have one of reasonable size, it is perfectly easy to use it to lift food out of the saucepan or the wok on to a serving plate.

Strainer

This is very useful for straining boiled noodles, blanched vegetables or excess oil from deep fried dishes. The traditional strainer is a round basket made of brass and steel mesh with a split bamboo handle, available in different sizes. It is less bulky to store than the average strainer and looks more interesting and decorative.

Sesame Chicken

Serves 4–6

3 lb (1.5 kg) fresh chicken
1 tablespoon (15 ml) corn oil
1 tablespoon (15 ml) Shaoshing wine **or** dry sherry
2 spring onions, cut into pieces 4″ (10 cm) long
4 slices peeled fresh ginger
salt, white pepper

Serving Sauce

1 tablespoon sesame seeds
2 teaspoons Szechuan peppercorns
½ teaspoon sesame paste
2 cloves garlic, creamed
½ teaspoon granulated sugar
¼ teaspoon salt
4 tablespoons (60 ml) corn oil
½ tablespoon (7.5 ml) sesame oil
3 tablespoons (45 ml) sweet chilli sauce
½ tablespoon (7.5 ml) light soy sauce
1½ tablespoons (22.5 ml) Shaoshing wine **or** dry sherry
2 pinches black pepper

Garnish

1 tablespoon chopped spring onion
2 teaspoons roasted white sesame seeds

Complementary dishes

Spring Onion Savoury (*page* 76)
Pork with Wooden Ears (*page* 24)
Peking Duck (*page* 54)

Wash and wipe dry the chicken and remove any fat around the tail end, then cut along the spine and split open from the middle of the back. Season it all over with 1 teaspoon of salt and 2–3 pinches of white pepper. Place it on a heat-proof shallow dish with half each of the ginger and spring onion on top and underneath the chicken. Pour over 1 tablespoon (15 ml) each of corn oil and Shaoshing wine to give flavour. Prepare your steamer or wok with steaming rack and place the dish over the boiling water. Steam at a constant high temperature for about 30–35 minutes, making sure there is always enough water in the wok (*see page* 14). The chicken should be only just cooked, to be perfect. Pour the natural juice from the chicken, which has gathered in the dish, into a container, to be used as stock in another dish – perhaps Drunken Fish (*page* 26). Let the chicken cool down completely.

Prepare the sauce as follows. First it is necessary to roast the sesame seeds in a pre-heated heavy pan (without any oil) at a high temperature until they turn golden.

Then put half of them, together with the Szechuan peppercorns, into a bowl or mortar and grind to a coarse powder with the end of the handle of a cleaver (*see page* 15), or a pestle. Add the sesame paste, sugar, salt, corn oil, sesame oil, sweet chilli sauce, soy sauce, Shaoshing wine, pepper and creamed garlic. Blend all the ingredients and set aside.

Fillet the cooked chicken and shred into matchstick-sized pieces. Arrange neatly on a serving dish, then pour some of the sauce over the centre of the meat and keep the rest to be served on the table. This is an extremely quick and easy dish to make. Best of all, the sauce can be made in a large quantity in advance and keeps for weeks in an airtight jar in the refrigerator. The chicken can be steamed and shredded ahead of time and wrapped in clingfilm, but the sauce should only be poured over the chicken just before serving.

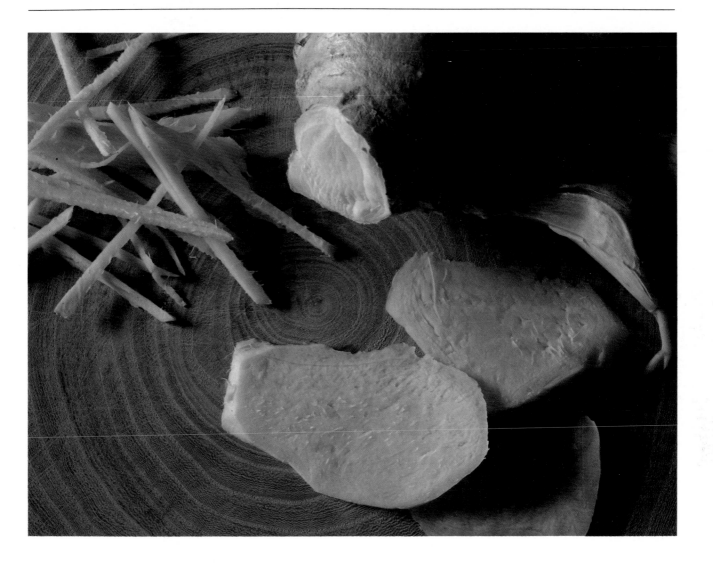

Ginger root is one of the most important spices in
Chinese cooking. It is normally used in conjunction with
garlic: the flavours complement each other without
overpowering the natural taste of the dish.

Szechuan Green Beans

Serves 4–6

1 lb (450 g) fresh green beans
2 oz (60 g) preserved cabbage
6 oz (180 g) pork
¼–½ teaspoon (1.25 ml–2.5 ml) chilli oil
1 tablespoon (15 ml) Shaoshing wine
½ teaspoon cornflour
3 cloves of crushed garlic
3 tablespoons chopped spring onion
1 tablespoon (15 ml) dark-coloured soy sauce
1 teaspoon granulated sugar
3 tablespoons (45 ml) corn oil
¼ teaspoon salt
2 pinches of white pepper

For this particular dish, it is possible to mince the pork in a mincing machine or food-processor, as the texture of the meat should be even and very fine. After mincing, marinate in soy sauce, cornflour, sugar and pepper and set aside in a bowl while you prepare the other ingredients.

Wash and dry the preserved cabbage and dice as small as possible. Place the dice in a small bowl. Next, top and tail the beans, wash them and blanch in slightly salted boiling water for 6–7 minutes. Drain in a colander.

Now, heat 1 tablespoon (15 ml) corn oil in a pre-heated wok at a high temperature and quickly stir fry the beans with ¼ teaspoon salt for 45 seconds. Transfer onto a pre-heated serving dish and keep warm. Finally, in the same wok, heat 2 tablespoons (30 ml) of oil, on a high temperature. Add the crushed garlic to flavour the oil, and press the pieces to extract as much juice as possible. Discard them when they are brown. Stir fry the pork quickly at a very high temperature for approximately 2–3 minutes, keep stirring to separate the pieces, add the cabbage, wine and chilli oil, and spring onions and stir a few more times.
Spread the sauce evenly over the beans, and serve.

Complementary Dishes

Paper Parcels (*page* 82)
Drunken Fish (*page* 26)
Stir-fried Chinese Cabbage (*page* 31)
Peking Duck (*page* 54)

Mincing is as important in Chinese cooking as
shredding (*shown on page* 41). With a sharp cleaver it
does not take long, and the texture is much better than
that of machine-ground mince.

Roast Beggar Chicken

Serves 4–6

3 lb (1.5 kg) fresh whole chicken
3 oz (90 g) shredded pork
2 oz (60 g) preserved cabbage
1 tablespoon (15 ml) corn oil
1 tablespoon (15 ml) Shaoshing wine **or** dry sherry
5 oz (150 g) bamboo shoot
salt
white pepper
1 large dried lotus leaf

Marinating ingredients

½ tablespoon (7.5 ml) dark-coloured soy sauce
1 teaspoon sugar
½ teaspoon cornflour

Soak the lotus leaf in lukewarm water for 2 hours. Rinse the preserved cabbage with cold water. Dry it with kitchen paper, then cut into shreds (*see page 21*) the size of matchsticks. Shred the bamboo shoot in the same way and set aside both vegetables in a bowl.

Next, mix the shredded pork with the soy sauce, cornflour, and sugar in a bowl, and leave it to marinate.

Heat 1 tablespoon (15 ml) of oil in a pre-heated wok on a high temperature. Stir fry the pork for 30 seconds, add the Shaoshing wine, stir fry briefly before adding the shredded cabbage and bamboo shoot. Then cook for about one more minute, stirring all the time.

Preheat the oven to 400°F/200°C/Gas 5. Remove any fat around the tail end of the chicken, after rinsing it with cold water. Pat dry with kitchen paper. Season with 1 teaspoon of salt and pepper all over (including the interior of the bird), and then stuff with the shredded mixture. Finally, wrap the entire chicken in the lotus leaf, and then wrap again with aluminium foil, sealing the edges carefully. Stand in a roasting dish, and roast for 40 minutes. Then turn down the heat to 325°F/160°C/Gas 3 for a further 40 minutes. The chicken should then be very tender.

Before serving, remove the aluminium foil; bring the chicken, still in its lotus leaf, to be unwrapped and served on the table.

Complementary Dishes

Transparent Noodles with Shrimps (*page* 88)
Chicken with Leek (*page* 96)
Beef with Fried Noodles (*page* 50)

Shredding is another of the basic techniques in Chinese cooking. Here bamboo is first sliced (along the grain, to preserve its texture), then cut into thin strips (again along the grain). Smaller pieces can then be made by chopping the shreds across.

Stir-Fried Prawns with Spring Onions

Serves 4–6

1 lb (450 g) medium-size uncooked Pacific or King Prawns
   (2–3″ (10 cm) long without the head is the perfect size)
3 oz spring onion
2 tablespoons coarse sea salt
1 teaspoon cornflour
½ teaspoon table salt
3 pinches of white pepper
1½ pint (850 ml) corn oil
2 slices fresh ginger, peeled
2 cloves garlic, crushed
½ teaspoon (2.5 ml) sesame oil
1 tablespoon (15 ml) Shaoshing wine **or** dry sherry

Utensils

a wok
a colander

First remove the heads and pull out the black alimentary canal. Then peel off the shells leaving the tails, and cut along the spine to half the depth of the body. The next step is to rub them all over with salt and leave for about 5 minutes before rinsing them again carefully with cold water to remove the salt. Dry them with kitchen paper, then leave them to marinate in a bowl with ½ teaspoon of salt, white pepper and cornflour.

Next, wash the spring onions and shake off the excess water before cutting them diagonally into thin slices, then place them in a small bowl.

Heat the oil in a wok at a high temperature for approximately 8 minutes and quickly deep fry the prawns for about 45 seconds. Transfer them with a slotted spoon into a colander and drain off the excess oil.

Pour away most of the oil from the wok, leaving about 2 tablespoons (30 ml). Heat the oil again, flavouring it with the ginger and the garlic and discarding them when they begin to brown. Quickly put in the prawns, stir fry for a few seconds before pouring in the Shaoshing wine or sherry and then add the spring onions and sesame oil and continue stir frying for a further 30 seconds, before serving on a pre-heated serving plate.

The total stir-frying process should not take more than 2 minutes.

Complementary Dishes
Spring Rolls (*page* 48)
Bean-Paste Chicken (*page* 46)
Stuffed Aubergines (*page* 108)
Stir-fried Seasonal Vegetables (*page* 31)

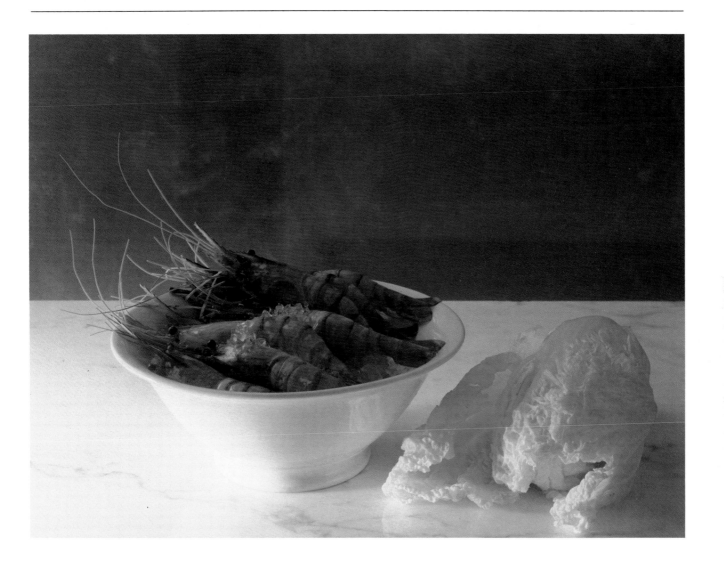

Sliced Pork with Wooden Ears

Serves 4–6

10 oz (300 g) pork tenderloin
3 oz (90 g) canned bamboo shoot
3 tablespoons wooden ears (form of dried mushroom)
1½ tablespoons (22.5 ml) light-coloured soy sauce
¼ teaspoon salt
2 pinches white pepper
1 teaspoon cornflour
4 tablespoons (60 ml) corn oil
1 tablespoon (15 ml) Shaoshing wine **or** dry sherry
2 tablespoons (30 ml) water
1–2 teaspoons granulated sugar
3 drops sesame oil
2 cloves crushed garlic
2 slices fresh ginger

Trim off any fat on the meat and slice into pieces approximately 2″ (5 cm) square and ⅛″ – ¼″ (3–6 mm) thick.

Place them in a bowl, marinate with 1 tablespoon (15 ml) soy sauce, sugar, cornflour, white pepper and leave them to be cooked later.

Soak the wooden ears in luke-warm water for half an hour. After soaking, it is necessary to wash the swelled wooden ears in a sink full of cold water to get rid of any grit. Keep rubbing them gently between fingers. Change the water two or three times. Eventually, let them float in a sink full of water for ten minutes. If there is any more grit left, it will drop to the bottom of the sink. After ensuring they are thoroughly clean gently lift the wooden ears out of the water and dry them with paper towels.

Slice the canned bamboo shoot along the grain (*see page 21*) into pieces approximately 2″ (5 cm) long, 1″ (2.5 cm) wide and ⅛″ (3 mm) thick. Put them together with the wooden ears.

Heat 1 tablespoon (15 ml) of oil in preheated wok on a high temperature, add 2 pinches of salt and quickly stir fry the bamboo shoot with the wooden ears for about 25 seconds. Replace them in a bowl.

On the same high temperature, heat 3 tablespoons (45 ml) of oil, seasoned with the ginger and the garlic, discard the pieces when they are slightly browned and quickly put in the meat. Keep stirring and separate any pieces that stick together. After one minute, add the water, Shaoshing wine, sesame oil, bamboo shoot and wooden ears, together with the rest of the soy sauce. Stir fry just for another minute and serve. The total cooking time, once the meat has been added, is approximately three minutes.

Complementary Dishes

Lemon Beef Soup (*page* 40)
Steamed Grey Mullet (*page* 92)
Prawns with Spring Onions (*page* 22)

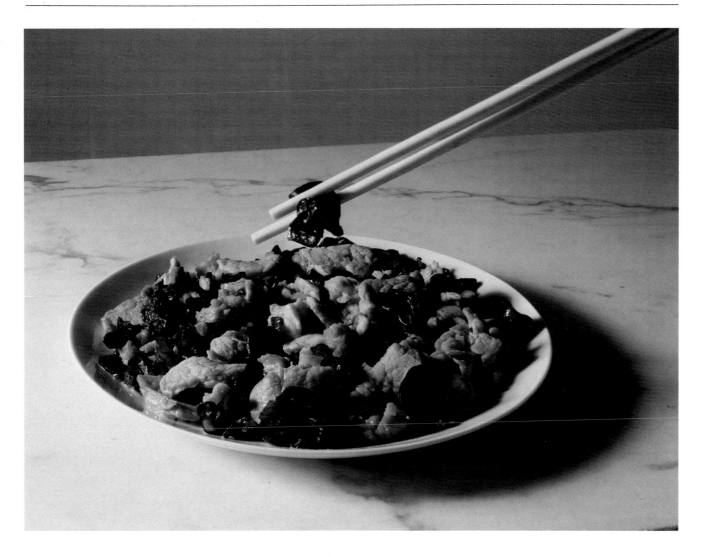

This is a Cantonese dish in which the contrast in both texture and colour of the ingredients is particularly striking.

Drunken Fish

Serves 4–6

1 lb (450 g) fillet of monkfish **or** cod steak **or** turbot
3 tablespoons (45 ml) Shaoshing wine **or** dry sherry
½ teaspoon salt
3–4 pinches of white pepper
1 pint (550 ml) corn oil
2 teaspoons cornflour mixed with
1 tablespoon (15 ml) cold water
1–2 teaspoons granulated sugar
2 thin slices of fresh ginger

To make the Stock

¾ pint (420 ml) water
1 lb (450 g) chicken bones **or** 1 lb (450 g) fish bones
¼ teaspoon salt
2 thin slices of fresh ginger

To make the stock, boil the water and add either chicken or fish bones (depending on what is available) together with the ginger. After one minute, turn down the heat to low, simmer the stock for approximately 45 minutes, or until the liquid has reduced to a quarter of a pint (140 ml), discard all bones and ginger and season with salt.

Wash the fish fillets and dry well with kitchen paper until there is no trace of wetness left on the paper, then cut them into pieces roughly 2″ (5 cm) square and about 1″ (2.5 cm) thick. Season with salt and white pepper.

Heat the corn oil on a high temperature and fry the two slices of fresh ginger. When they are browned after approximately 45 seconds, remove from oil, then quickly put in the fish, keeping the high temperature, separate any pieces that stick together and fry for about 40 seconds. Turn off the heat, remove with a slotted spoon and place in a strainer, then leave them over a bowl to drain any excess oil. Empty most of the oil from wok, leaving only 2 tablespoons (30 ml) to cook the sauce with.

On a high temperature again, put in Shaoshing wine, stock, sugar and wet cornflour mixture, bring to the boil, but keep stirring as it thickens.

Gently place the fish into the sauce, cook for approximately 40 seconds and serve on a pre-heated shallow dish.

Complementary Dishes

Sesame Chicken (*page* 16)
Spring Onion Savoury (*page* 76)
Lion's Head (*page* 28)
Plain Boiled Rice (*page* 27)

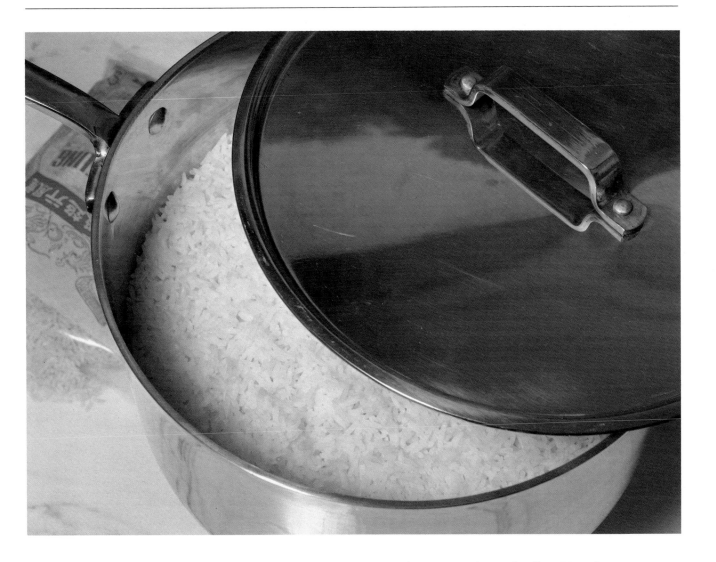

To cook rice correctly: wash 1 lb (400 g) rice to remove dust and starch; use a 7–8″ (20 cm) saucepan and fill with cold water, stir the rice with your hand and pour the water away slowly. Repeat this 4–5 times. The rice will then be quite clean. Add cold water to ¾″ (2 cm) above the rice and put on a high heat with the lid on. When the water has come to the boil, turn down to medium heat and place the lid askew. When all the water has disappeared from the top of the rice, replace the lid and turn the heat down very low for a further 20 minutes. *Do not stir.*

Lion's Head

Serves 4–6

Cut the meat into cubes or strips, then cut again smaller and finally chop with a sharp cleaver until you have small uneven pieces (*see page* 19). The end result should be similar to mince but do *not* attempt to save time by buying mince, as the quality and texture will be inferior.

Mix the meat with all the ingredients listed for the meatballs, and let it marinate for an hour. Wash and cut the Chinese cabbage into 3″ (7.5 cm) pieces lengthwise and place in a bowl. Form the meat into three equal-sized balls. Heat 2 tbs (30 ml) oil to a high temperature in a frying pan and fry the meat balls on both sides for five minutes, until lightly browned. Take care to keep the shape intact. Remove and place them in a sandpot (*see page* 14). Add all the ingredients for the sauce and simmer for 25 minutes on a very low heat. Heat 1 tablespoon (15 ml) corn oil with a pinch of salt and stir fry the Chinese cabbage for 1 minute, in a pan. Do not brown. Remove the meatballs from the sandpot, place the fried cabbage at the bottom of the sandpot, return the meatballs, and cook for a further 5–6 minutes before serving. If you are using a saucepan, transfer the contents to a shallow serving dish, retaining the cabbage at the bottom with the meatballs on top.

You will agree with me that this dish should be prepared ahead of time. It will save some of the effort and time of cooking another dish for a dinner party. However, do remember not to cook the cabbage until just before this dish is needed, so it will taste and look perfect.

Ingredients for the Meatballs

1 lb 6 oz (650 g) lean pork tenderloin with about
   2 oz (60 g) pork fat
6 canned water chestnuts, chopped
3 spring onions, chopped (white part only)
1½ tablespoons (22.5 ml) rice wine (saké) **or** cooking
   sherry
1 small lightly beaten egg
2 teaspoons cornflour
1½ teaspoons finely chopped peeled ginger
1½–2 teaspoons sugar
¼ teaspoon white pepper
½ teaspoon salt
2 tablespoons (30 ml) corn oil

½ lb (250 g) Chinese cabbage
3 tablespoons (45 ml) corn oil

Ingredients for the Sauce

½ pint (225 ml) chicken **or** pork clear stock
1 teaspoon cornflour mixed with 1 tablespoon (5 ml)
   cold water
1 teaspoon sugar
3 teaspoons (15 ml) light-coloured soy sauce
4 teaspoons (20 ml) saké, **or** cooking sherry

Complementary Dishes

Wun-Tun Soup with Watercress (*page* 34)
Stir-fried Chicken with Broad Beans (*page* 72)
Plain Boiled Rice (*page* 27)

A typical Shanghai dish.

Smoked Quail

Serves 4

4 fresh quail **or** frozen if fresh are not available
2 tablespoons (30 ml) corn oil

For the Marinade

1 tablespoon (15 ml) maltose (malt sugar) **or** golden syrup or honey
3 tablespoons (45 ml) dark-coloured soy sauce
1 tablespoon (15 ml) sweet chilli sauce **or** tomato sauce
2 cloves of star-anise
½ teaspoon five spice powder
1 clove of crushed garlic
1 tablespoon (15 ml) cooking wine **or** sherry

To Smoke

2 tablespoons China tea

Dressing the serving dish

4–6 spring onions carved into flowers
watercress

To make the spring onion flowers, cut off the root then cut off the green part leaving a whole spring onion 3″ (7.5 cm) long. Criss-cross both ends with a sharp knife leaving 1″ (2.5 cm) uncut in the centre. Submerge in iced water and the ends will curl outwards. Keep in cold water until required.

Skin and clean the quail. Place in a bowl with the mixed marinade ingredients for 2–3 hours.

Preheat the oven to 400°F/200°C/Gas 6. Heat the oil in a wok or frying pan for 1–2 minutes, on a high temperature. When it starts to smoke, cook the quail for approximately 7–10 minutes all over but especially on the breast side where the meat is thicker. Turn the heat down a little if the quail appear to be burning. Remove and place on a baking tray in the middle of the hot oven for a further 10 mins. The quail will now be cooked.

Put the tea leaves in a clean dry wok or large saucepan. Place a wire rack over them and cover. Turn the gas up high for approximately 1 minute or until the tea starts to smoke. Quickly remove the lid and place the quail on the rack, replace the lid and smoke for approximately 30 seconds.

Serve on a dish garnished with the spring onion flowers and watercress.

Complementary Dishes

Stir-fried Lamb with Green Peppers (*page 78*)
Stir-fried Cabbage (*see opposite*)
Fresh Steamed Scallops (*page 94*)

Stir-fried Chinese cabbage is an easy and tasty accompaniment to dishes like Smoked Quail or Braised Leg of Pork (*page* 36). Wash the cabbage and shake it dry, cut it into strips about 2″ (5 cm) wide. For 1 lb (450 g) cabbage, heat 2 tablespoons (30 ml) corn oil to a medium temperature, fry two thin slices of ginger (discard when they start to colour). Add cabbage and ½ teaspoon salt, fry for about 7 minutes. Stir constantly. Turn heat down if oil gets too hot: it is important not to discolour the cabbage.

Jung

Makes 14

2 lb (900 g) glutinous rice
12 oz (360 g) pork belly rashers (skinless)
1 tablespoon (15 ml) dark-coloured soy sauce
1 teaspoon cornflour
3 oz (90 g) bamboo shoot (canned)
3 Chinese mushrooms (dried)
1 teaspoon sugar
¼ teaspoon five spice powder
1¼ teaspoon salt
3 pinches of white pepper
14 dried shrimps (optional)
25 dried bamboo leaves

Soak the bamboo leaves in a bowl of cold water for a few hours until they are flexible. Shake off excess water.

Soak the Chinese mushrooms in hot water in a bowl for half an hour, then drain. Remove the stems of the mushrooms, squeeze out excess water, then cut into thin slices. Soak the dried shrimps in a separate bowl. Drain and rinse with cold water, drain again and set aside.

Cut the pork rashers into 1″ (2.5 cm) pieces and marinate for about half an hour with soy sauce, cornflour, sugar, ¼ teaspoon salt, white pepper and the five-spice powder. Wash the rice several times with cold water. Drain and place in a bowl with one teaspoon of salt, mixed in well.

Select a bamboo leaf, making sure it has no splits in it and trim off approximately 2″ (5 cm) from each end. Now bend the leaf in the middle and form into a cone.

Take another leaf, cut it in half and slide the narrower end down inside the cone on the opposite side to the ends of the first. Trim off the end of the leaf with scissors to the same height as the others, holding the cone firmly in one hand. Place approximately 1 tablespoon of rice in the bottom to form a bed, lay on top of this 3 pieces of meat, 3 pieces of mushroom and one each of the bamboo shoot and shrimps, then cover with more rice and pack down.

To close the cone, fold in the three ends to overlap one another, and completely cover the rice. This will produce a pyramid shaped parcel, which should then be bound tightly and tied with hemp or string to hold it together.

Place the parcels in a steamer over a high temperature, wait until the water starts to boil, then turn down the heat to low and steam for about 6 hours.

Once the Jung are cooked, they can be kept fresh in a refrigerator for several days. Steam again for an hour before eating. Serve with a little soy sauce and chilli sauce. Do not eat the bamboo leaves!

... The unusual recipe may at first seem very difficult to to make but you will find it very easy after the first few tries. The cooked rice takes on an amazing flavour from the bamboo leaves. Its origins are described on page 7.

Wun-Tun Soup with Watercress

Serves 4–6

For the Wun-Tun

¾ lb (350 g) sifted plain flour
3 large eggs (beaten)
2 tablespoons (30 ml) cold water
¾ teaspoon salt
cornflour
8 oz (250 g) tenderloin **or** fillet of pork
2 oz (60 g) finely chopped tinned bamboo shoots
2 pinches of white pepper
¾ teaspoon salt
1 large egg, beaten
½ teaspoon cornflour
1 tablespoon finely chopped spring onion (white part only)
¼ teaspoon sugar

Ingredients for making the Soup

3 lbs (1.5 kg) chicken carcasses
2 slices of fresh ginger
3–3½ pints (2 litres) hot water
1–1½ teaspoons salt
2 bunches of watercress
2 tablespoons chopped spring onion

Complementary Dishes

Sweet and Sour Wun-Tun (*page* 56)
Bean Paste Chicken with Peppers (*page* 46)
Stir-fried Seasonal Vegetables
Fried Rice with shrimps (*page* 52)

First prepare the broth. Boil the chicken carcasses in the water for 5 minutes. Skim off the scum. Add the ginger and salt and simmer gently for 1½–2 hours. Remove the carcasses and ginger and check the seasoning.

Mince the pork (*see page* 19) without any fat, and place in a bowl. Add 1 tablespoon of chopped white part of the spring onion, and the chopped bamboo shoots, mixed together with salt, pepper, sugar, 1 tablespoon of beaten egg and the cornflour.

Put the sifted flour into a large bowl, add the salt, beaten eggs and cold water. Mix together clockwise with a fork until it forms a large ball. Continue kneading with the palms of your hand until it becomes smooth and pliable. (It should be very bouncy). If the dough seems to be a little bit wet, dust it with a sprinkling of flour but ensure it is not sticky. Work for a further 5 minutes and divide into 3 balls. Place in a bowl with a little cornflour on the bottom to prevent them sticking, and cover with a damp cloth. Remove one ball at a time and roll out on a well cornfloured surface until it is paper-thin, cut into 3″ (7.5 cm) squares and make the Wun-Tun as illustrated on page 77. It is always useful to make a few more skins than needed as they can be kept fresh in the refrigerator, individually dusted with cornflour and wrapped in cling film or foil.

Cook the ready made Wun-Tun in slightly salted boiling water for about two minutes, to remove any flour dust, then drain in a colander. Remove any skin or fat from the partly cooked Wun-Tun. Put into cold water and bring to the boil again. Drain. The second boiling ensures they are properly cooked.

Heat the broth. Add the sprigs of watercress, 2 tablespoons of chopped spring onion, the Wun-Tun, and cook for 1½–2 minutes before transferring to a tureen to serve.

Braised Leg of Pork

Serves 4–6

2–2½ lb (1 k–1.25 kg) leg **or** shoulder of pork
(with the skin)
3 thin slices of onion
2–3 tablespoons (30–45 ml) light-coloured soy sauce
1 tablespoon (15 ml) golden syrup
8 oz (250 g) Chinese cabbage
¾ pint–1 pint (425–550 ml) hot water
3½ tablespoons (52.5 ml) corn oil
2 slices fresh ginger
2 cloves crushed garlic
½ teaspoon five spice powder
salt
1 teaspoon cornflour mixed with
1 tablespoon (15 ml) water

In a little muslin bag

1–2 whole star anise (or the equivalent in broken pieces)
1 tablespoon Szechuan peppercorns
½ tablespoon whole black peppercorns

Wipe the pork with kitchen paper and score the skin with diagonal cuts approximately ½″ (1.25 cm) apart, then repeat in the opposite direction to form a criss-cross pattern on the surface.

Preheat a wok over a medium temperature, and pour in 1 tablespoon (15 ml) of corn oil, stir fry the onions with a pinch of salt until transparent but not brown. Then place in a bowl. Next, using the same pan, put in 2 tablespoons (30 ml) of oil with the garlic and ginger, then heat to a high temperature and add the piece of pork. Fry for about 3 minutes to seal and brown it, keeping the scored skin uppermost.

Empty the entire contents of the wok into a sandpot (or a saucepan), add the onions, the soy sauce, syrup, five spice powder, the bag of spices, and finally the water. Bring to the boil for 2–3 minutes, then turn the heat to low and simmer for 3–3½ hours, until the meat becomes tender when pierced with a fork. Add extra water if the liquid reduces too much. It should measure just under ½ pint (275 ml).

When the meat is cooked, thicken the sauce a little with the wet cornflour mixture.

Wash and cut the Chinese cabbage into four rounds (as illustrated), place two at each side of the meat and cook for a further ten minutes. Remove the spice bag, then serve, or alternatively, transfer the meat onto a shallow serving dish. Place the cabbage slices round it, and then pour the sauce over the top.

Complementary Dishes

Chicken in Plum Sauce (*page* 38)
Prawns with Ginger (*page* 90)
Plain Boiled Rice (*page* 27)
Seasonal Vegetable

The flavour of this dish is greatly improved if it is left for a few hours after being cooked. I think this is a perfect choice for a dinner party, with the advantage that it can be prepared ahead of time.

Chicken in Plum Sauce

Serves 4–6

1 lb 4 oz (550 g) breast of chicken (without bone)
5 dried Chinese mushrooms
4 oz (120 g) tinned bamboo shoot
1–2 teaspoons granulated sugar
2 tablespoons (15 ml) dark-coloured soy sauce
2 tablespoons (30 ml) plum sauce
salt
white pepper
1 teaspoon cornflour
3 tablespoons (45 ml) corn oil
2 tablespoons (30 ml) water
2 tablespoons (30 ml) Shaoshing wine **or** dry sherry

To serve with

1 large Cos, Webbs or Iceberg lettuce
6 tablespoons (90 ml) plum sauce

Wash and toss the lettuce, keeping it crisp and fresh. Soak the Chinese mushrooms in boiling water, strain, squeeze out any further water, dice into tiny pieces (*see page* 41) smaller than ⅛″ (3 mm) square. Also dice the bamboo shoot into tiny pieces and set both aside in separate bowls.

Wash the chicken breasts and dry with kitchen towels. Slice and then dice them the same size as the bamboo shoot. Marinate the chicken dice in a bowl with 1 tablespoon (15 ml) soy sauce, cornflour, sugar, plum sauce and 1 tablespoon of Shaoshing wine, leaving it to absorb the seasoning for half an hour.

Next, put 1 tablespoon (15 ml) of corn oil in a pre-heated wok on a high temperature, stir fry the diced bamboo shoot for a few seconds and then add the diced mushrooms. Add 2 pinches of salt and white pepper and cook for 30 seconds, then empty the mixture into a bowl. In the same wok, heat 2 tablespoons (30 ml) of oil and, when it is hot, quickly stir fry the chicken, separating the tiny pieces as best as you can. Cook for one minute. Keeping the same temperature add remaining soy sauce and Shaoshing wine, as well as the water. (Keep stir frying all the time.) Then finally, add the cooked bamboo shoots and mushrooms. Cook for approximately one more minute and taste a little to test the seasoning before serving.

To present this dish correctly, you should spoon some of the chicken mixture onto a piece of lettuce, placed in the palm of one of your hands, spoon a little plum sauce over the chicken mixture (the amount is entirely up to you) and then, holding the lettuce leaf firmly with both hands like a shallow cup, you eat it. It is advisable to provide finger-bowls.

Complementary Dishes
Paper Parcels (*page* 82)
Braised Leg of Pork (*page* 36)
Traditional Fried Noodles (*page* 50)

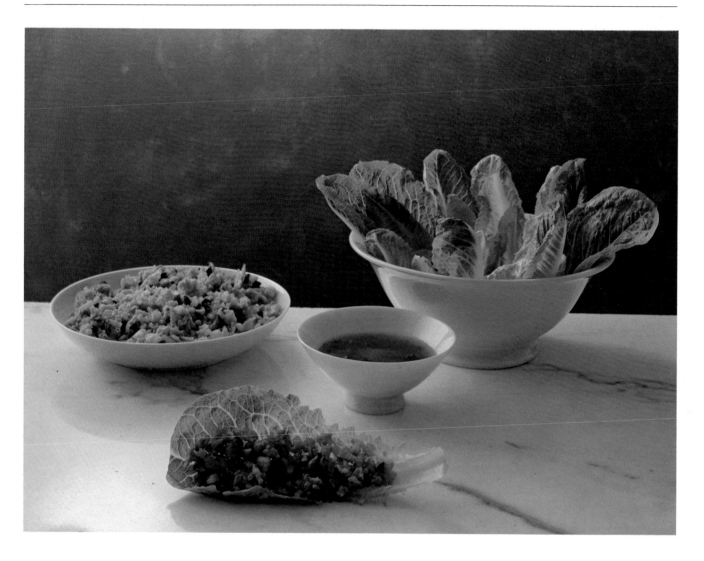

This is a Peking dish. You can use lettuce in this way also as a substitute for pancakes in Peking Duck (*page* 54).

Lemon Beef Soup

Serves 4–6

1 lb 4 oz (550 g) stewing beef **or** shin
3 thin slices Spanish onion
fresh lemon juice
fresh lemon peel
3 teaspoons (15 ml) light soy sauce
4 pints (2.25 litres) water
a pinch of sugar
1½ teaspoons salt
3 pinches of white pepper
¼ pint (150 ml) chicken stock (*optional*)
2 spring onions

Wash and dry the meat and trim off all the fat. Then cut into 2″ (5 cm) chunks and season with 1 teaspoon of salt, the sugar and white pepper, all together in a bowl. Bring the water to the boil in the saucepan, empty in the entire bowl of meat, together with the onion slices. Simmer on a low heat for one hour.

Cut the lemon in half and squeeze out all the juice. Then put half of the peel into the soup, and cook for half an hour. Add the lemon juice, remove the lemon peel and simmer for another hour.

Finally, add salt and sugar and taste for correct seasoning. When the soup is reduced to one third of the liquid, add the chicken stock (if available), colour with soy sauce and put in the sliced spring onions. Cook for a further ten minutes. The total cooking time should be between 2½–3 hours.

This Cantonese soup is very simple soup to make, and can be cooked ahead of time. It will give you a good appetite as a starter.

Complementary Dishes

Sesame Chicken (*page* 16)
Drunken Fish (*page* 26)
Szechuan Green Beans (*page* 18)
Plain or Fried Rice (*pages* 27 or 52)

Basic methods of cutting all sorts of meat. Slicing is always done very thinly, so that the meat will require very little cooking time in methods like stir-frying. Shredding is done by cutting the thin slices lengthwise. Dicing is done for stir-frying where the meat gets marinated first. The meat is cut into strips about ½″ (or 1 cm) wide, then crossways into squares.

Yam Noodles

Serves 4–6

8 oz (250 g) yam noodles
12 oz (350 g) pork tenderloin
3 thin slices of Spanish onion
3 tablespoons (45 ml) dark-coloured soy sauce
1–2 teaspoons sugar
3 tablespoons (45 ml) corn oil
1 fresh chilli (optional)
2–3½ tablespoons (30–50 ml) hot water
1 oz (30 g) coriander **or** celery leaf
2 cloves of crushed garlic
2 slices of fresh ginger
1 teaspoon cornflour
salt
2 pinches of white pepper
6 tablespoons (90 ml) stock, lightly seasoned

Soak the yam noodles in cold water for about half an hour and then empty into a colander. Rinse them with half a kettleful of hot water and set aside. Wash and dry the coriander or celery leaf and chop coarsely. Set aside in a bowl.

Wash the piece of pork fillet and dry it with kitchen paper. Then cut into slices ⅛″ (2 mm) wide across the grain. Marinate with 1 tablespoon (15 ml) of soy sauce, half of the sugar, cornflour and 2 pinches of white pepper, for half an hour. Now, heat 1 tablespoon (15 ml) of oil in a pre-heated wok on medium heat. Add a pinch of salt, stir fry the onion for 20 seconds and empty into a bowl. In the same wok, heat 2 tablespoons (30 ml) of oil on a high temperature, season it with the ginger and garlic, discarding them after 30 seconds (keep turning and pressing to extract the maximum flavour). At the same temperature stir fry the pork, adding the rest of the soy sauce, sugar, the chilli, if used, and the noodles. Continue to cook for one minute, then add the stock and water, cook again for approximately 5–6 minutes. (Taste a piece of noodle, it should not be either too chewy or too soft in texture.) Then finally add the onion and the coriander or celery leaf, stir fry a few more times and the dish is ready to be served.

Complementary Dishes

Stuffed Fillet of Sole (*page* 84)
Stir-fried Mangetout Peas and Chinese Sausage (*page* 60)
Chicken with Leeks (*page* 96)
Stir-fried Cabbage (*page* 31)

Stir-fried Scallops
Serves 4–6

1 lb 4 oz (570 g) fresh scallops
6–8 small gloves of garlic
1 tablespoon finely chopped spring onion
2–3 pinches white pepper
¼ teaspoon salt
½ tablespoon Shaoshing wine **or** dry sherry
½ tablespoon (7.5 ml) light-coloured soy sauce
a pinch granulated sugar
2 tablespoons (30 ml) corn oil

Separate the white flesh of the scallops from the roes and trim off any brownish veins. Leave the scallops whole unless they are very large. Rinse them well and allow to drain on kitchen paper for at least half an hour to ensure that they are dry enough to brown properly. Just before you are ready to cook the scallops, put them in a bowl and season with the salt and pepper.

Peel and trim the cloves of garlic. Heat the oil in a pre-heated pan or wok, and fry the garlic for about one minute, or until it is golden brown. Check that the oil is really hot, and then add the scallops and their roes. Let them brown thoroughly, and after about two minutes add the wine, soy sauce and sugar. Stir fry for one minute and add the spring onion. Stir a few more times and transfer the entire contents of the pan to a heated serving dish. Eat immediately. The total cooking time should not exceed 3½ minutes after you have added the scallops.

This must be one of the easiest and quickest of dishes to cook, and the scallops and garlic taste absolutely delicious.

Complementary Dishes
Wun-Tun Soup (*page* 34)
Chicken with Pickled Vegetables (*page* 66)
Lion's Head (*page* 28)
Seasonal Vegetables

Bean Paste Chicken with Green Peppers

Serves 4–6

1 lb (450 g) breasts of chicken (without bone)
5 oz (150 g) fresh green peppers, sliced
1 teaspoon (5 ml) dark-coloured soy sauce
1 tablespoon crushed yellow bean paste
1 teaspoon (5 ml) sweet chilli sauce
1 tablespoon (15 ml) Shaoshing wine **or** dry sherry
1 teaspoon granulated sugar
1 pint (550 ml) corn oil
2 pinches of white pepper
¼ teaspoon salt

Trim off any skin or fat from the chicken, dice into irregular 1″ (2.5 cm) cubes, season with salt and white pepper then place in a bowl.

Mix in another bowl the soy sauce, sweet chilli sauce, Shaoshing wine, sugar and crushed yellow bean paste. Pour the corn oil into a wok and heat on a high temperature. Once it is hot, turn off the heat for the moment.

Take out 2 tablespoons (30 ml) of hot oil, put it into a pre-heated frying pan, add the green peppers with a pinch of salt and quickly stir fry for about 35 seconds. Remove from the oil and place in a bowl.

Turn on heat for the wok and once the oil is hot again, quickly deep fry the meat for 20 seconds, remove with a slotted spoon, place in a strainer.

Now, turn on the heat for the frying pan, pour in the bowl of sauce mixed earlier, bring to the boil, quickly put in the chicken, separating any pieces that stick together, add the green peppers, then stir fry for about 30 seconds, making sure all the chicken is well covered by the sauce and serve.

Complementary Dishes

Spinach Parcel Soup (*page* 102)
Stuffed Fillet of Sole (*page* 84)
Beef with Black Soy Beans (*page* 64)
Plain Boiled or Fried Rice (*page* 27 or 52)

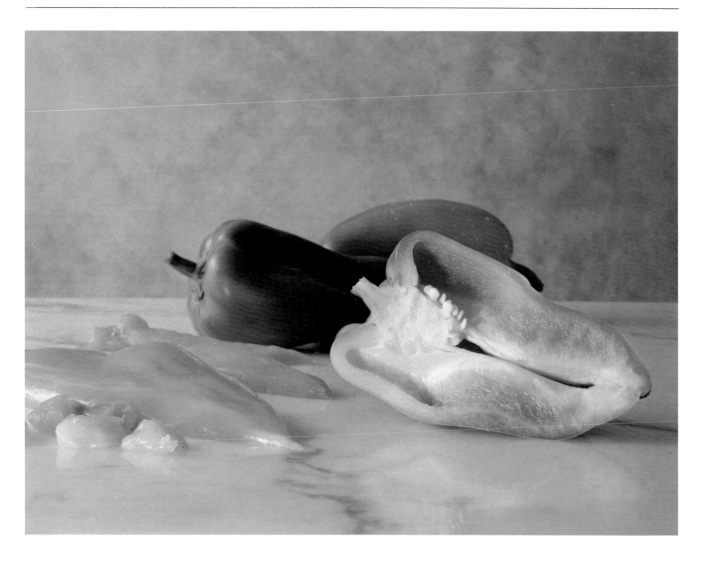

In Chinese cooking, the freshness and visual appeal of the basic ingredients is just as important as the finished dish.

Spring Rolls

Makes 18

10 oz (300 g) pork tenderloin **or** escalope
1 lb (450 g) fresh bean sprouts
3 dried Chinese mushrooms
2 spring onions
1 tablespoon (15 ml) dark-coloured soy sauce
1 teaspoon granulated sugar
¾ teaspoon salt
2 pinches of white pepper
4 tablespoons (60 ml) corn oil
1 teaspoon cornflour
2 slices fresh ginger
2 cloves crushed garlic
1 packet (20 sheets) spring-roll skins
1 beaten egg
1 pint (550 ml) corn oil

Complementary Dishes

Lemon Beef Soup (*page* 40)
Drunken Fish (*page* 26)
Cantonese Pork Fillet (*page* 86)
Stir-fried Chinese Cabbage (*page* 31)

The filling

Soak the Chinese mushrooms in boiling water for at least half an hour, discard the stems, cut into slices ⅛″ (3 mm) thick. Wash and cut the spring onions diagonally into slices ⅛″ (3 mm) thick. Wash the bean sprouts and dry with kitchen paper. Shred the pork into match-stick size pieces (*see page* 41) place in a bowl and add soy sauce, cornflour, sugar and white pepper, mix well together and marinate for about half an hour.

Heat 2 tablespoons (30 ml) of oil in pre-heated wok on a high temperature, add salt. Once the oil is hot, stir fry the bean sprouts for about 1½ minutes and empty into a bowl. In the same wok, heat the rest of the oil for 40 seconds, season with fresh ginger and garlic which must then be removed. Put in the meat, stir fry for one minute, pour in the juice only from the bean sprouts, add the mushrooms and spring onions, then cook for further one minute, finally add the bean sprouts and stir fry for approximately 30 seconds.

Empty the contents into a bowl and leave to cool down before making up the spring rolls as shown below.

Making the Spring Rolls

1. Take 1 piece of spring-roll paper.
   (Spring-roll paper should be kept in the refrigerator but when you are using it, leave at room temperature for at least 2 hours or until pliable).
2. Put a small amout of cooked mixture in one corner.
3. Fold over the corner, then take the left-hand corner and the right-hand corner and hold all three together and roll to the opposite side – as illustrated.
4. Brush the last corner with a little beaten egg to seal the parcel together.
5. Place rolls on a cornflour-dusted plate until it is time to fry them.
6. Heat the oil at high temperature. It must be hot enough to fry immediately. Fry until golden in colour. Strain then drain well on kitchen paper.

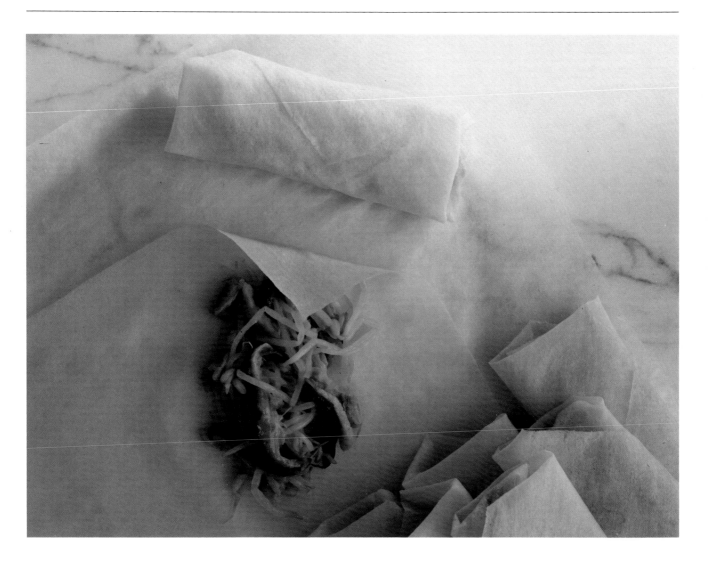

This is a Cantonese dish which can be prepared well ahead of time. It has its variants through all of South East Asia, and has long become a firm favourite in the Western world as well.

Beef and Green Peppers with Fried Noodles

Serves 4–6

8 oz (250 g) fillet **or** sirloin of beef
1 tablespoon salt
2 pinches white pepper
2 slices fresh peeled ginger
2 cloves crushed garlic
8 oz (250 g) thin egg noodles
4 oz (120 g) green peppers
1 tablespoon fermented and salted black soy beans
   (*optional*)
4 oz (120 g) sliced Spanish onion
½ teaspoon salt
3 tablespoons (45 ml) dark-coloured soy sauce
2 teaspoons cornflour
4 tablespoons (60 ml) corn oil
1 tablespoon (15 ml) Shaoshing wine **or** dry sherry
8–9 tablespoons (130 ml) hot water
2 teaspoons sugar

Complementary Dishes

Steamed Scallops (*page* 94)
Chicken with Broad Beans (*page* 72)
Stir-fried Seasonal Vegetable
Fried Rice with Fresh Shrimps (*page* 52)

Bring 3 pints (1.75 l) of water to the boil with 1 tablespoon of salt. Cook the egg noodles for about 2 minutes, drain them in a colander and rinse under the cold tap for a few seconds. Shake off the excess water before laying them out on kitchen paper to dry for at least 2–3 hours.

Wash and dry the pieces of beef and cut into thin slices (*see page* 41), place them in a bowl and marinate with 2 tablespoons (30 ml) of soy sauce, pepper, 1 teaspoon of sugar and half of the cornflour. Cut both the onions and the green peppers into 1″ (2.5 cm) square chunks. Place them in separate bowls. Mix 2 tablespoons (30 ml) of soy sauce, 1 teaspoon of sugar and the remaining cornflour with enough hot water to make a thinnish sauce. Reserve.

Heat a non-stick frying pan at a high temperature, fry half of the noodles for 1–2 minutes or until the outer ones are crisp (turn down the heat a little to prevent burning). Keep turning over while you fry. Then transfer to a heated serving plate and keep it in a cool oven while you cook the rest of the noodles in the same way. Leave them all in the oven until the meat and the sauce are ready.

Heat 2 tablespoons (30 ml) of oil in a preheated wok at a high temperature. Stir fry the onion for 25 seconds before adding the green peppers and ½ teaspoon of salt. Stir fry for another 25 seconds and transfer all into a bowl.

In the same wok, heat another 2 tablespoons (30 ml) of oil, with the garlic and the ginger, which must be removed from the oil once they have flavoured it. Then quickly add the black soy beans; stir fry a few times before adding the beef and Shaoshing wine. Stir fry for 45 seconds before returning the green peppers and the onions, again stir fry for a further 30 seconds. Spread the meat and vegetables in an even layer on top of the fried noodles, leaving a border of uncovered noodles. Pour the cornflour mixture into the still-hot wok, stir a few times to prevent the cornflour settling in the bottom, bring to the boil and pour over the dish and serve.

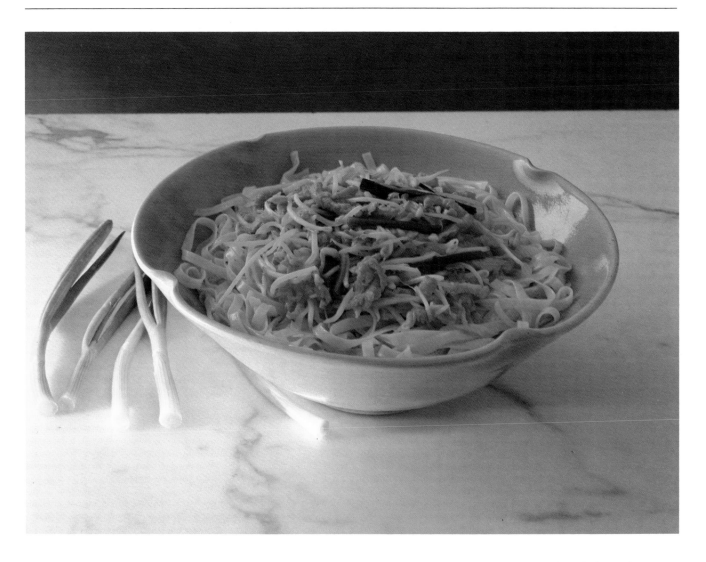

Noodles, stir-fried together with shredded bamboo shoots and bean sprouts, are accompaniment for meat and other dishes as are fried or plain boiled rice (*pages 52 and 27*).

Fried Rice

Serves 4–6

10–12 oz (300–360 g) boiled long grain rice
6–8 oz (180–250 g) small/medium cooked prawns
  (peeled)
5 tablespoons (75 ml) corn oil
2 oz (60 g) frozen peas
1 beaten egg
2 teaspoons salt
4 oz (120 g) diced onion

With a fork, fluff up the boiled rice to ensure that it is free from lumps. Heat half the oil over medium heat and quickly stir fry the rice with 1 teaspoon salt for 1½ minutes (this can be done in a non-stick frying pan if available). Very quickly, pour the beaten egg evenly all over the mixture, turn heat down and blend with a spatula or fork. The egg must be quickly absorbed by the rice and to achieve this you need to blend it extremely fast, avoiding pieces of egg being cooked separately as in scrambled eggs. After approximately 2 minutes the rice should be an even pale yellow in colour.

Wash the prawns and dry them in kitchen paper to absorb all excess water. Peel and dice the onions ¼″ – ⅛″ (5–2½ mm) square. Rinse the frozen peas under hot water and drain well. Heat the remaining oil moderately and stir fry the onion with ½ teaspoon salt for approximately 1 minute, or until the onion becomes transparent. Do not brown. Turn the heat up and add the prawns, stirring constantly for approximately 30 seconds, then add the well drained peas and the other ½ teaspoon salt and stir a few times just to mix the ingredients evenly. There should be less than one tablespoon of juice in the bottom of the wok at this stage. Add the rice to the mixture and stir fry for approximately 30 seconds. Taste and serve.

Fried rice should not be too dry but served shining and moist. It can be prepared before your guests arrive, but do not cover with a lid until it is quite cold, or it would make it damp and sticky by the condensation. To re-heat it only takes approximately a few minutes of stir frying on medium heat.

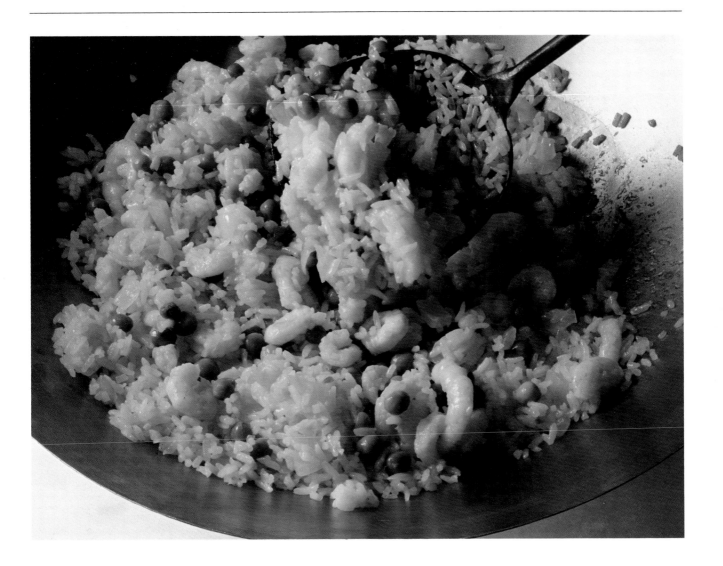

Peking Duck

Serves 4–6

4–4½ lb (1.5–2.25 kg) duck
2 tablespoons (30 ml) maltose **or** honey **or** golden syrup
1 teaspoon (5 ml) Shaoshing wine **or** cooking sherry
4 tablespoons (60 ml) hot water
½ tablespoon (7.5 ml) light-coloured soy sauce
a pinch of red powder (food colouring)

To serve with

6 tablespoons (90 ml) Hoi Sin sauce (fresh sea sauce)
8 spring onions
½ cucumber
10–12 pancakes

To make Pancakes

4 oz (120 g) plain flour
¼ pint (150 ml) boiling water
½ tablespoon (7.5 ml) corn oil
1 pinch salt

Complementary Dishes

Wun-Tun Soup with Watercress (*page* 34)
Steamed Trout or Bass (*page* 80)
Stir-Fried Chinese Cabbage (*page* 31)
Fried Rice (*page* 52)

Preparing and cooking the Duck

Wash and clean the duck removing any fatty lumps from around the vent. Sprinkle a couple of pinches of salt inside the carcass. Hold the duck over a sink and pour a kettle full of boiling water over the skin to enable you to pluck out any remaining bits of feathers. (This process will also clean and open the pores and will make the skin colour quickly and evenly as it roasts). Hang in an airy place for a few hours (anything between 4 and 12 hours). Mix the maltose with the wine or sherry, soy sauce, red powder and hot water and coat the duck all over with a pastry brush while is is still hanging. Repeat this treatment every hour for 2–3 hours and leave hanging overnight which will make the skin nice and crispy. Preheat the oven the oven to 400°F/200°C/Gas 6. Prick the skin of the thighs, back and lower breast. Hang the duck from a hook on the top shelf over a tray, or place on an open wire rack. Roast for approximately 80 minutes. *Do not baste.* If it seems to brown too much too soon turn down to 375°F/190°C/Gas 5, but roast for an extra 5 minutes.

Preparing the Vegetables

Wash and dry the spring onions and cucumber. Cut the spring onions into 4″ (10 cm) lengths, cut in half then shred lengthwise. Cut the cucumber into 4″ (10 cm) pieces, then halve each piece lengthwise and discard the seeds. Now cut each half lengthwise down the centre giving you four equal 4″ (10 cm) strips. Slice paper-thin and finally shred lengthwise, as shown in the picture. You should now have thin cucumber strips 4″ (10 cm) long (some will have a rind and some will not). Divide the spring onions and cucumber into two equal portions and place on two serving plates (as illustrated).

To make the Pancakes

Pour the boiling water into the sifted flour, add the oil and stir constantly for approximately 2–3 minutes. The mixture will become a soft and bouncy dough. Divide into two equal parts. Make rolls approximately 4″ × 1″ (10 × 2½ cm) and cut each roll into four pieces. Roll out on a well floured surface into 6″ (15 cm) paper-thin

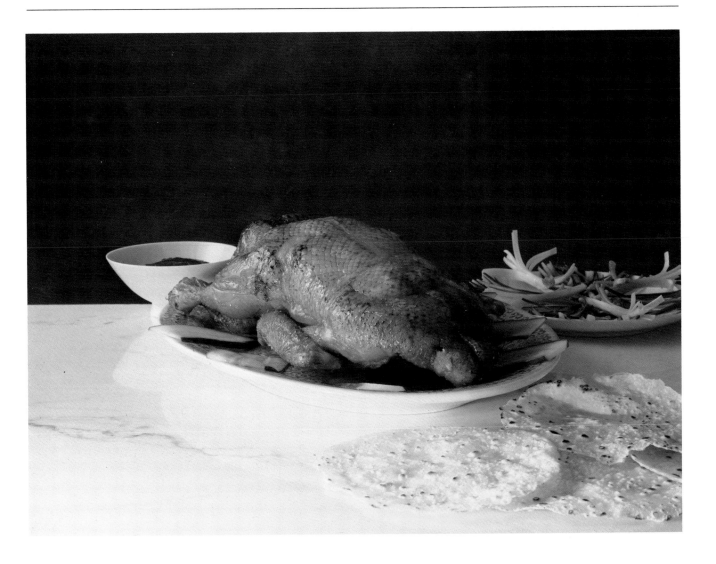

To serve

circles and fry individually for 30 seconds on each side on a low to medium heat, taking care not to burn them. It is advisable to make the pancakes when the duck is cooking, but ensure they are well wrapped in clingfilm and stored in the refrigerator to keep them fresh. Ten minutes before serving your Peking Duck, steam the pancakes a few at a time on a rack in a wok for approximately five minutes. Wrap a cloth around the lid to absorb the steam, which will otherwise make the pancakes soggy.

Place all your ingredients on the table with the Peking Duck as a centrepiece, garnished with watercress, spring onion or slices of cucumber. Each guest takes a pancake and places two slices of duck in the centre with some spring onion and cucumber and a little Hoi Sin sauce spread evenly over it, rolls the pancake with their fingers and eats. Traditionally, the duck is carved away from the table and served off the bone. However, I prefer to serve it on the table as this keeps it hot and moist and is also time-saving – apart from being fun. Try to ensure that all your guests have a piece of the skin as this is the true delicacy.

Fried Sweet and Sour Wun-Tun

Serves 4–6

Ingredients for the Wun-Tun
see page 34
1½ pints (850 ml) corn oil

Ingredients for the Sauce

4 oz (120 g) tinned pineapple rings
3 oz (90 g) Spanish onion
3 oz (90 g) sweet green peppers
1 teaspoon (5 ml) sugar
½–1 tablespoon (7.5–15 ml) malt vinegar
2–3 tablespoons (30–45 ml) sweet chilli sauce
3 tablespoons (45 ml) corn oil
½ teaspoon salt
2 pinches of white pepper
1–1½ teaspoons cornflour mixed with water
generous half pint (330 ml) pineapple juice diluted
    with water

First cook the Wun-Tun as described for Wun-Tun Soup (*see page* 34). The prepare the rest of the ingredients as follows. Cut each pineapple ring into four. Deseed and slice the green pepper into thin rings, and cut the onion into 1″ (2.5 cm) square chunks. Mix the pineapple juice and water with the cornflour in a cup and add the sweet chilli sauce and the sugar as well.

Next, deep fry the Wun-Tun before cooking the sauce. Using a wok, on a high temperature, heat 1½ pints (850 ml) of corn oil. When the oil is hot, quickly put in The Wun-Tun and cook until they turn golden brown, remove them with a slotted spoon into a colander, then place them on some kitchen paper to get rid of any excess oil. Transfer them onto a wire rack and put in a low oven, to be served later with the sweet and sour sauce.

Reheat 3 tablespoons (45 ml) of oil from the deep-frying on a high temperature, put in the salt and pepper, stir fry the onion slices for about 30 seconds, taking care not to let them get brown, then add the green peppers and cook for further 20 seconds. Finally, add the pineapple chunks and the pineapple juice mixture to the wok and keep stirring until the sauce thickens. When it begins to bubble, it is ready. Place the Wun-Tun on a deep serving dish and pour the sauce over them.

Complementary Dishes

Sesame Chicken (*page* 16)
Spring Onion Savoury (*page* 76)
Steamed Grey Mullet (*page* 92)

Toffee Apples and Bananas

Serves 4–6

2 medium-size eating apples
2 just-ripe bananas
1 beaten egg
3 tablespoons plain flour
3 tablespoons cornflour
a pinch of salt
4 tablespoons (60 ml) water
2 tablespoons roasted sesame seeds
1½ pints (850 ml) corn oil for deep frying

Ingredients for the Toffee

1 lb (450g g) caster sugar
½ pint (275 ml) cold water
a pinch of cream tartar
a bowl of cold water for setting the toffee

Sift the plain flour and cornflour together, add the beaten egg, a pinch of salt and the water and mix into a thick creamy batter. Peel and core the apples and cut each into six pieces. Peel the bananas, cut into four pieces. Dip the apples and bananas into the batter and deep fry in hot oil, turned down immediately, for approximately two minutes or until golden in colour. Remove from the oil, strain in a colander, and keep warm.

Over a constant high temperature dissolve the sugar in water, with the cream of tartar. Cook in a saucepan for approximately 20–25 minutes or until it starts to turn golden. Remove the toffee from the heat, place it, in its saucepan, in a large bowl of hot water to stop it from setting. Have ready a second bowl of iced water.

Dip each piece of fruit separately into the hot toffee and then quickly into the iced water to set the toffee.

To spin the toffee as shown in the photograph, there are two methods: a) Dip a pair of chopsticks 1″ (2.5 cm) deep in the toffee, raise them above your head and let the toffee drip off the end in thin strings or threads, as it sets, forming an attractive pattern evenly over the dish. b) Cut the curved bottom of a wire whisk with wire cutters leaving the straight sections and dip into the toffee and quickly twirl in the air over the dish. (This would only be worthwhile if you plan to make this recipe frequently.)

Finally, sprinkle with sesame seeds and serve.

I think it is a good idea to serve some exotic fruits to your guest to fill up the time while you are preparing the toffee apples and bananas (*see pages* 71 and 111).

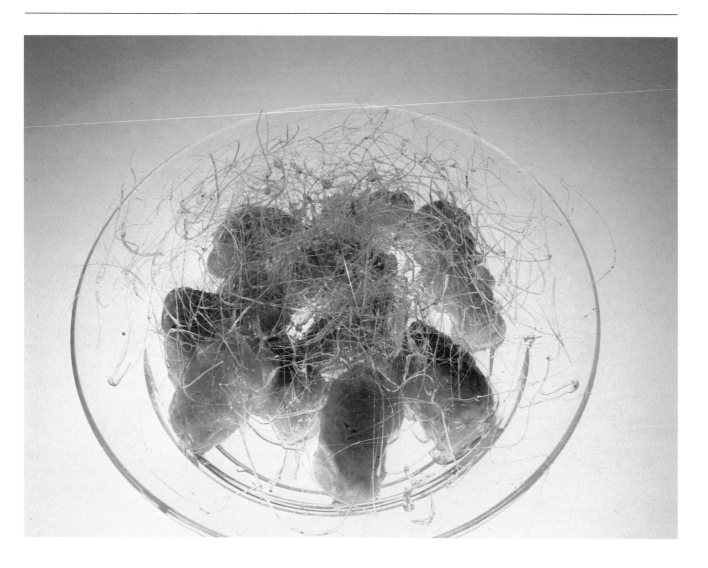

Chinese toffee apples are quite unlike their Western
fairground namesakes.

Stir-fried Mangetout Peas and Chinese Sausage

Serves 4–6

12 oz–1 lb (360–450 g) thin mangetout peas
   (approximately 2–3″ long (5–7.5 cm))
4 Chinese pork, liver **or** beef sausages
½ teaspoon salt
3 tablespoons (45 ml) corn oil

Chinese sausages are a truly traditional delicacy eaten mostly during the winter season and they are frequently given as a present when they first arrive on the market. Amongst other specialities, they are often eaten during the Chinese New Year. They are traditionally only available during the winter months as they are difficult to keep fresh when the temperature rises and also too rich to eat when the weather is hot. As the climate is cooler in Europe we are able to enjoy this dish nearly all the year round as sausages are easily found in any Chinese supermarket. Likewise, mangetout peas can now be obtained for more than six months of the year.

Place the sausages on a plate on a rack in the wok over water and steam on a high gas for a few minutes with the lid on. (A bamboo steamer is preferable if you have one.) When the fat becomes transparent remove them from the steamer and slice diagonally very thinly and keep warm. Pull off the stalks, tails and any attached strings from the mangetout. Wash them and drain in a colander. On a fairly high heat, heat the oil and stir fry the mangetout with the salt for approximately two minutes, taking care *not to scorch* them, turning the heat down if necessary. Mangetout should not be undercooked as they may have a 'rusty' taste, but it is equally important not to overcook them as it is essential that they remain green and crisp. Because they have a high sugar content they can easily burn, therefore temperature and timing must be flexible.

Add the sliced sausages and stir a few times to mix thoroughly and heat the sausage through. Taste and serve.

Complementary Dishes

Cantonese Pork Fillet (*page 86*)
Sliced Pork with Wooden Ears (*page 24*)
Seasonal Vegetable
Transparent Noodles with Dried Shrimps (*page 88*)

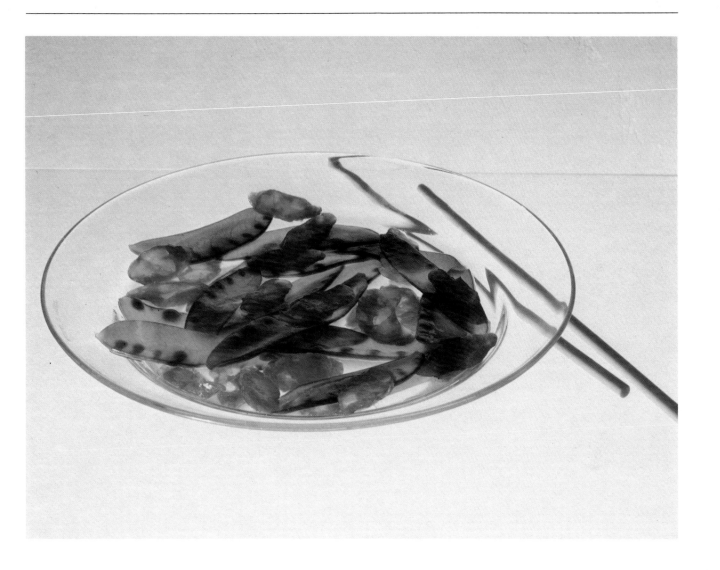

Boiled Noodles

Serves 4–6

8 oz (225 g) noodles
2 teaspoons salt
2½ pints (1.5 litres) water

Put the salt in boiling water, add the noodles and cook for approximately 2–3 minutes, stirring constantly to avoid them sticking together. (Do not turn the heat down.) Strain and run under a cold tap for a few seconds to stop them cooking further. If you are going to fry them, leave them on a plate for 2–3 hours to dry. If you are going to eat them with an already prepared soup, do not rinse but serve immediately after boiling.

This boiling time is for ⅛″ (3 mm) noodles, but if you are using a thinner variety they should take about 1 minute less to cook.

There are many types of Chinese noodles and just as many styles of cooking them. All but the very tasty shrimp-flavoured ones are eaten as an accompaniment to meat, poultry, fish or vegetables, either fried (*see page* 50) or in a good clear stock.

Beef with Black Soy Beans

Serves 4–6

1 lb (450 g) fillet **or** porterhouse beef steak
½ lb (225 g) fresh French beans
5–6 oz (150 g) Spanish onions
1 tablespoon dried **or** tinned black soy beans
6 tablespoons (90 ml) corn oil
½ teaspoon cornflour
1½–2 teaspoons sugar
1 tablespoon (15 ml) Shaoshing wine **or** cooking sherry
2 pinches salt and pepper
1 clove crushed garlic
2 slices peeled ginger root
2 tablespoons (30 ml) dark-coloured soy sauce
1 tablespoon (15 ml) cold water

Top and tail the French beans and boil in one pint of slightly salted cold water for approximately 3–4 minutes but ensure they remain crispy. Slice the beef thinly *across the grain*, remove any fat and marinate with soy sauce, sugar, salt, pepper and cornflour for ½ hour. Cut the onion into 1″ (2.5 cm) chunks and stir fry with a little salt in 2 tablespoons (30 ml) oil on a moderate heat for approximately two minutes, do not brown. Add the blanched beans and cook for 30 seconds. Place in a bowl. In the same wok, heat the remaining oil to a high temperature, fry the garlic and ginger for a few seconds to flavour the oil and then discard them. Add the dried or drained tinned soy beans to the hot oil, stir for a couple of seconds, add the beef and quickly stir fry for approximately 2 minutes according to how well you like beef cooked, still on a high temperature. When almost cooked, add the wine, 1 tablespoon (15 ml) cold water, French beans and onions. Cook for a further minute and serve.

Complementary Dishes

Spare Ribs (*page* 106)
Stir-fried Chinese Cabbage (*page* 31)
Lion's Head (*page* 28)
Plain Boiled Rice (*page* 27)

Black soy beans are fermented and have a strong salty taste. The tinned variety are less strong.

Chicken with Pickled Vegetables

Serves 4–6

10 oz (300 g) shredded breast of chicken, off the bone
4 oz (120 g) canned pickled cabbage
6 oz (180 g) canned bamboo shoots
1 teaspoon cornflour
2 teaspoons sugar
6 tablespoons (90 ml) corn oil
2 tablespoons (30 ml) water
2 tablespoons (30 ml) light-coloured soy sauce
salt and pepper

Shred chicken into thin long pieces (*see page* 41), discard any fat and skin. Place in a bowl and marinate with soy sauce, sugar, cornflour, 1 tablespoon (15 ml) corn oil, a pinch of white pepper and ½ teaspoon salt. Leave to one side. Shred the bamboo shoots to a similar size as the chicken (*see page* 21). Always remember to cut the bamboo shoots *along the grain*. Rinse pickled vegetables in cold water and dry with paper towel. Chop into very small pieces, between ⅛"–¼" (3–6 mm). Heat 2 tablespoons (30 ml) oil to a high temperature in a preheated wok and stir fry the bamboo shoots with a pinch of salt for approximately 40 seconds, add the pickled vegetables and cook for a further 30 seconds Place in a bowl. Using the same wok, heat the remaining oil to a high temperature and quickly stir fry the chicken for approximately 2 minutes, add the water, bamboo shoots and pickled vegetables and stir fry a few more times or approximately one minute. Add more sugar and salt if desired.

It is very easy to cut the pickled vegetables very small by holding a few pieces together firmly between your thumb and index finger, and running the cleaver along at ⅛" (3 mm) intervals.

Complementary Dishes

Fried Sweet and Sour Wun-Tun (*page 56*)
Szechuan Green Beans (*page 18*)
Prawns with Spring Onions (*page 22*)
Peking Duck (*page 54*)

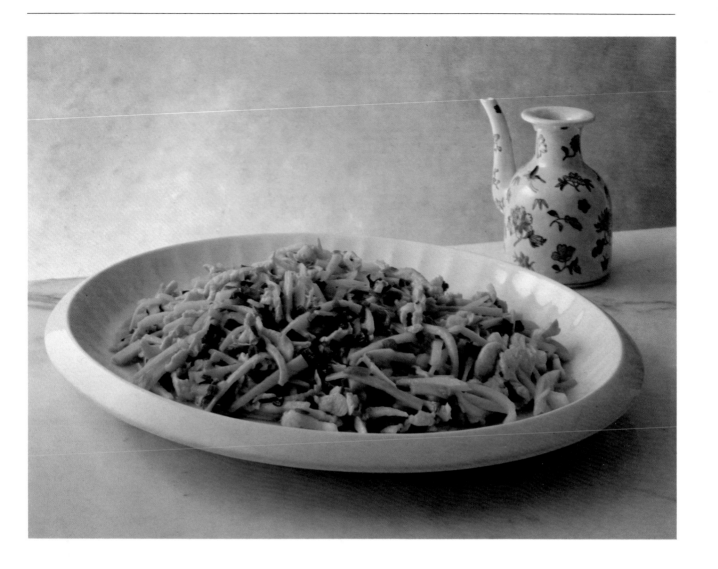

Deep-fried Spicy Rolls

Makes 28

8 oz (250 g) minced beef
2 oz (60 g) Spanish onion
3 oz (90 g) spring onion
1 oz (30 g) Chinese parsley (fresh coriander)
2 oz (60 g) finely minced preserved cabbage
7 sheets of spring-roll paper
1 small fresh chilli, finely sliced **or** ¼–½ teaspoon
   of chilli oil
¼ teaspoon five spice powder
1 tablespoon (15 ml) dark-coloured soy sauce
2 tablespoons (30 ml) corn oil
1–2 teaspoons granulated sugar
½ teaspoon cornflour
1 clove garlic
salt
2 pinches of white pepper
2 slices of fresh ginger
1 beaten egg
1½ pints (850 ml) corn oil

Finely chop both the Spanish onions and the spring onions and place them in separate bowls. Peel the dried skin off the garlic and cream it by scraping with a knife in a sprinkle of salt. Mince the beef (*see page* 19 or in this case it is perfectly adequate to buy top-quality ready-minced beef) and marinate the meat with soy sauce, cornflour, sugar and white pepper in a bowl.

Heat 1 tablespoon (15 ml) of corn oil in a pre-heated wok at a medium temperature. Stir fry the Spanish onion for 20 seconds and then add the spring onion and chilli. Cook for just another 10 seconds and then transfer them into a bowl.

In the same wok, heat another tablespoon (15 ml) corn oil at a high temperature and stir fry the beef with the ginger and garlic for about 25 seconds, and then add the chopped preserved cabbage. Stir fry just a few more times and add the onion mixture as well as the chopped Chinese parsley, and the five spice powder. Give a few more stirs and then transfer everything into a bowl. Allow to cool in the refrigerator for a couple of hours.

Cut each sheet of the spring-roll paper into four approximately 4″ (10 cm) square pieces. Spoon a teaspoonful of the mixture into a corner of a square, fold it using the same method as for the making of spring rolls (*see page* 48). Do not forget to seal each parcel with a little beaten egg, using a pastry brush. The size of each finished parcel is about 2″ (5 cm) long and just a little smaller than 1″ (2.5 cm) in diameter. Finished parcels should be put on a flour-dusted plate until needed for frying.

Heat 1½ pints (850 ml) of corn oil in a wok at medium to high temperature, and deep fry the parcels a few at a time until they turn golden all over. Let them drain on kitchen paper. These parcels can also be served as a snack with drinks.

Complementary Dishes

Steamed Trout or Sea Bass (*page* 80)
Smoked Quail (*page* 30)
Lamb with Green Peppers (*page* 78)
Fried Rice (*page* 52)

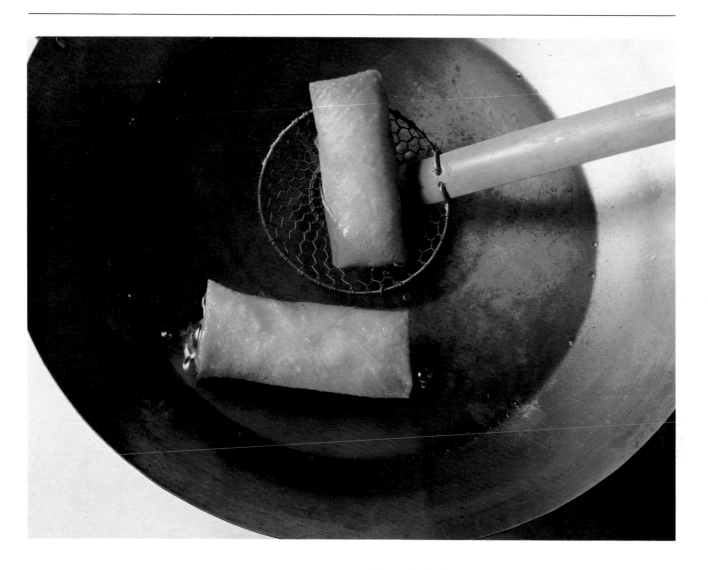

The method of making these tasty parcels is illustrated on page 49.

Lin-Go

1 lb (450 g) glutinous rice
1 lb (450 g) natural Chinese brown sugar in slabs **or**
  medium brown soft sugar
1¼ pints (700 g) water
2 tablespoons (30 ml) corn oil

Rinse the rice a few times with cold water in a bowl and leave it soaking in cold water overnight. Drain the rice in a colander before putting one third of it with ⅓ pint (200 ml) of water to liquidise until you have a white powdery liquid. Pour the contents of the liquidiser into a muslin bag and squeeze out all excess water. Empty the ground rice into a bowl. Repeat the same procedure until all the rice has been ground, and all the water has been discarded. Melt the sugar (broken into small pieces) with ¼ pint (150 ml) of water, at a medium to high temperature, and mix together with the ground rice, adding the syrup little by little to obtain a smooth paste. Use a wire whisk to get rid of any odd lumps before pouring into a shallow non-stick baking tin.
Place the steaming rack in the centre of the wok. Fill wok with boiling water to just below the rack. Place the baking tin on the rack and steam with a lid at a moderate temperature for 1 hour. Then turn the heat to low and steam for another 20 minutes.

Let the cake stand for a few hours, off the heat, before lifting it out of the baking tin. Just before you want to serve the Lin-Go cut part of it into ¼″ (6 mm) slices according to how many guests you have. Two thin slices should be enough for one person. The remainder can be kept in a cool place for a few days. Heat the oil in a frying pan to a high temperature and fry on both sides until brown, or even slightly burnt. Transfer them to a serving plate.

This type of cake is eaten traditionally during the Chinese New Year (*see page* 8), but it is now included among the many Dim-Sum lunch dishes (*see page* 10). It can also be eaten as a snack at teatime or suppertime.

Dried and preserved fruit (not always sweet but sometimes spicy or even sour) are eaten much as chocolate or candy are in the West. In this picture, outside the plate are dried persimmon; on the plate (clockwise from the large crystalized figs at the top): liquorice Hua-Mei (prunes), Chuan-Pei lemon, another fig, Kum Quat (like tiny Clementines), and liquorice olives. In the middle of the plate are preserved prunes.

Stir-fried Chicken with Broad Beans

Serves 4–6

10 oz (300 g) shelled fresh **or** frozen broad beans
9 oz (270 g) breast of chicken
salt
2 pinches white pepper
2 slices fresh ginger
2 cloves garlic, crushed
1½ pints (850 ml) corn oil
1 tablespoon (15 ml) Shaoshing wine **or** dry sherry
1 teaspoon (5 ml) granulated sugar
½ teaspoon cornflour
1 tablespoon (15 ml) light-coloured soy sauce

First wash the chicken breasts and dry with kitchen paper. Dice (*see page* 41) into small pieces of roughly the same size, but of uneven shape, and then marinate in a bowl with salt, pepper, cornflour, soy sauce and sugar.

Shell and skin the broad beans, and leave them aside in a bowl. Heat the oil in a wok at a high temperature, and when it is hot add the garlic and ginger, press them with the wok-stirrer to extract the juice and remove when brown. Empty all the chicken into the pan for just 15 seconds. Then quickly remove with a slotted spoon into a colander. Empty out all the oil except for two tablespoons (30 ml). Stir fry the beans at a high temperature for about 30 seconds, and then quickly add the fried chicken and the Shaoshing wine. Stir fry for another 10 seconds and serve in a pre-heated serving plate.

Complementary Dishes

Paper Parcels (*page* 82)
Stuffed Aubergines (*page* 108)
Grey Mullet with Lemon (*page* 92)
Beef and Green Peppers with Fried Noodles (*page* 50)

Stir frying is the most common and most important method of Chinese cooking. It is done in oil flavoured with garlic and ginger. Correct preparation of the ingredients is essential, cooking time is minimal due to the small size of the prepared ingredients, and the natural flavour of each individual bit is sealed in and preserved. The dish shown is stir-fried chicken with cashew nuts, a favourite restaurant dish made in much the same way as the recipe opposite.

My Cake

Makes 12

Ingredients for the pastry

8 oz (250 g) sifted plain flour
8 tablespoons (120 ml) hot water
4 tablespoons (60 ml) melted hot lard
2 pinches salt
1 teaspoon icing sugar
1½ pints (850 ml) corn oil for deep frying

Ingredients for the filling

4 oz (120 g) roasted peanuts
2 oz (60 g) demerara sugar
or
12 tablespoons (180 ml) sweet crushed black beans
or
12 tablespoons (180 ml) sweet chestnut cream

Pour the lard and the hot water (which should be freshly boiled) into a mixing bowl into which you have sifted the flour and salt, and stir with a fork quickly in a clockwise direction until it has gathered into a mass. Knead lightly a few times until it just holds together and remains bouncy and pliable. It should be slightly damp but not sticky. Leave one half in the bowl under a damp cloth, and prepare the other half as if you were making puff pastry. This is done by dusting a work surface and a rolling-pin with some flour, rolling out the pastry into a rectangular sheet, folding one third over from both ends. Then roll it out again. Repeat this process 3 times; keep sprinkling a little flour each time to prevent the pastry from sticking.

Finally, after the pastry has been rolled out into a rectangular shape again, cut into 6 pieces 4″ (10 cm) square. Repeat the same method with the remaining half of the dough. Place all the pieces of pastry back into the mixing bowl, and cover again with a damp cloth while making up the little cakes.

To make the peanut filling chop the peanuts coarsely with an electric blender or food-processor, and mix well together with the sugar in a bowl. Place 1½ tablespoons (22.5 ml) of this mixture in the centre of a piece of the pastry, fold and seal the edges diagonally in exactly the same way as the recipe for Spring Onion Savoury (*see page* 76). Alternatively, use 1 tablespoon of either sweet crushed black beans or chestnut cream as the filling.

Heat the oil in a wok at a high temperature, deep fry each cake until it turns golden. Stand on a cake rack to get rid of any excess oil.

Let them cool down a little before dusting lightly with icing sugar. These cakes can be served either hot or cold.

Chinese people are fond of sweet cakes for their
festivals. This photograph shows a typical Chinese cake
but the recipe given opposite is one I have invented
myself. The pastry is simple and delicious; it can also
be used for Spring Onion Savory (*next page*).

Spring Onion Savory

Makes 4

8 oz (250 g) finely chopped spring onion
6 oz (180 g) Spanish onion
½ teaspoon salt
2 pinches white pepper
1½ pints (850 ml) corn oil

Ingredients for the pastry

8 oz (240 g) plain flour
8 tablespoons (120 ml) boiling water
4 tablespoons melted lard
⅛ teaspoon salt

Complementary Dishes

Sesame Chicken (*page* 16)
Prawns with Ginger (*page* 90)
Beef and Green Pepper with Fried Noodles (*page* 50)
Smoked Halibut (*Page* 104)

Dice the Spanish onion approximately ⅛" (3 mm) square. Heat 2 teaspoons (10 ml) of corn oil at a medium heat and stir fry the onion for about 1½ minutes. Turn down the heat if necessary to prevent the onion browning. Transfer into a medium-sized bowl, and add the uncooked spring onion with the ½ teaspoon (2.5 ml) of salt and the pepper.

To make the pastry, sift the flour into a large mixing bowl with the salt, pour in the hot melted lard and the boiling water (allow to cool for a few seconds first), then very quickly and vigorously stir the mixture in a circle with a fork until it turns into a softy bouncy dough. Knead the dough only three or four times and divide into four portions. Bring out one at a time and keep the rest in the same bowl, covered with a damp cloth to keep them moist.

Now, sprinkle plenty of flour on a work-top and rolling-pin. Roll the dough into a rectangular shape. Fold in a third from each end and roll together into another rectangular shape (the same way as you would when making puff pastry). Repeat the folding three times, but the last time, roll the pastry into a square shape and trim to four 6" (15 cm) squares with a knife. Place a quarter of the onion mixture in the centre and close by lifting the corners and folding them diagonally into the centre. Seal by pressing the seams together, and then twisting the seam edges with a finger and thumb to make a pretty scalloped pattern. Now, you will have a very attractive pastry parcel about 4" (10 cm) square.

Repeat the process to make the rest of the parcels. Heat the oil in a wok at a high temperature, then deep fry two parcels at a time, turning them so that they brown evenly. Remove them with a fish slice or slotted spoon and place on kitchen paper to remove excess oil. Transfer to a cake rack and keep warm in the low oven until they are ready to be served.

Cut into 4 squares to serve.

Many Chinese dishes are wrapped up in squares of pastry of different varieties (*see pages* 35, 49, 57 *and* 69). For example, this photograph shows the correct way of folding the small skins used for making Wun-Tun (*page* 34).

Stir-fried Lamb with Green Peppers and Pancakes

Serves 4–6

10 oz (300 g) fillet of lamb
1 tablespoon light-coloured soy sauce
1 teaspoon cornflour
5 oz (150 g) green pepper
4 oz (120 g) spring onions
a few slices of fresh chilli (*optional*)
2 teaspoons granulated sugar
1 tablespoon (15 ml) Shaoshing wine **or** dry sherry
3 tablespoons (45 ml) corn oil
1 teaspoon salt
2 pinches white pepper
2 cloves garlic, crushed
2 slices fresh ginger

pancakes – allow one to two pancakes per person

Remove any veins and fat from the lamb and cut into thin slices across the grain. Place them in a bowl and marinate for half an hour in the soy sauce, sugar and cornflour.

Cut the green pepper in half and remove all the seeds before cutting into thin slices about ⅛″ (3 mm). Likewise, cut the spring onion diagonally to a similar thickness. Place them in separate bowls.

Make the pancakes (*see page 54*). Keep them hot in a steamer, off the heat. Wrap a tea-towel round the saucepan or steamer lid so it can absorb the moisture and prevent the pancakes becoming soggy.

Next, heat 1 tablespoon (15 ml) of oil in a pre-heated wok. Stir fry the green pepper and the chilli for 20 seconds before adding the spring onions and cook for another 20 seconds. Transfer them all into a bowl to be used later.

In the same wok, heat the rest of the oil with the ginger and garlic, discarding the pieces after 30 seconds. Quickly empty the meat into the hot oil. Stir fry for about a minute. Add the Shaoshing wine or sherry, then return the green vegetables to the wok. Again stir fry all together for just over another minute and serve with the steamed pancakes. The guests wrap a spoonful of the cooked lamb in a pancake and eat it with their fingers.

Complementary Dishes

Steamed Trout or Sea Bass (*page 80*)
Braised Leg of Pork (*page 36*)
Stir-fried Cabbage (*page 31*)
Fried Rice (*page 52*)

Steamed Trout or Sea Bass

Serves 4–6

1 lb 4 oz (550 g) fresh trout **or** sea bass
3 Chinese dried mushrooms (*optional*)
2 oz (60 g) spring onion
6 thin slices fresh ginger, peeled
3–4 pinches white pepper
2 tablespoons (30 ml) corn oil
1 tablespoon (15 ml) light-coloured soy sauce
salt

Wash the spring onions and shake off excess water, then trim off the ends before cutting diagonally into approximately ⅛″ (3 mm) thick slices. Place them in a corner of a small plate. Shred the fresh ginger slices into thin match-sticks (*see page* 21), place them in another corner of the same plate. Soak the Chinese mushrooms in hot water with a lid on for at least half an hour, remove stems and cut evenly into four or five slices. Leave an end on each slice attached at the under-side to form a fan shape. (This is a common decoration in Chinese cookery.) Set them aside with the spring onion and ginger until later.

Wash the fish and dry with plenty of kitchen paper, then season inside and out with salt and pepper.

Place the fish on a shallow heat-proof serving dish. Score the top of the fish 2 times or alternatively cut ¼–½″ (6–12 mm) deep along the spine. Both of these methods of preparing the fish will help it to cook quicker. Place the mushrooms equally along the surface of the fish, and distribute the spring onion and the ginger evenly in between.

Finally, sprinkle the corn oil and the soy sauce over the entire fish.

Heat some water in the bottom of a wok with a steaming rack. When the water begins to boil, place the dish containing the fish onto the steaming rack, cover with a tight-fitting lid and steam at a constant high temperature for about 8 minutes. Then it is ready to be served.

Be careful not to overcook the fish as you will spoil it. The liquid which collects in the dish forms a delicious sauce which is spooned over the fish before serving.

Complementary Dishes

Cantonese Pork Fillet (*page 86*)
Chicken with Pickled Vegetables (*page 66*)
Stir-fried Cabbage (*page 31*)

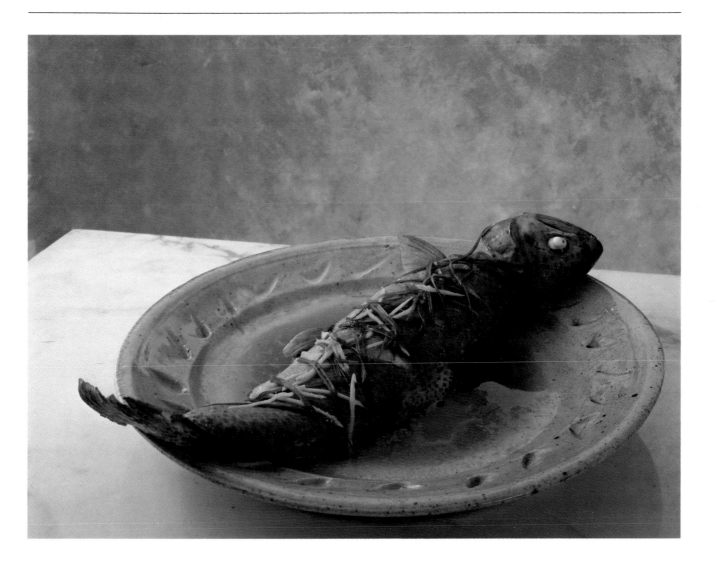

This classic Cantonese method is indeed one of the best and simplest ways to cook a fresh fish.

Paper Parcels

Makes 14

8 oz (250 g) pork tenderloin
8 oz (250 g) breast of chicken
leaves from 7 stalks of Chinese parsley (coriander)
2½ tablespoons (37.5 ml) dark-coloured soy sauce
1 teaspoon (5 ml) sesame oil (or corn oil if you prefer)
1 teaspoon granulated sugar
1 teaspoon cornflour
1½ pints (850 ml) corn oil
2 pinches white pepper

14 pieces greaseproof paper 6″ by 10″ (15 cm by 25 cm)

Cut the fourteen pieces of greaseproof paper (a roll is most convenient) and fold in half lengthwise.

Cut the chicken and the pork across the grain into ⅛″ (3 mm) thick slices approximately 2″ (5 cm) square, place them in separate bowls and marinate each with half of the soy sauce, sugar, cornflour and the white pepper. Leave for at least half an hour.

To make the parcels. First, brush the papers at the point where the meat will be placed (*as illustrated*) with a thin coat of sesame or corn oil (this will help to prevent the meat sticking to the paper as well as adding an interesting nutty flavour). Divide the two fillings between the papers and then place a sprig of Chinese parsley on those with the chicken filling so that you can identify the different flavours after the parcels are cooked.

After making sure the two ends of the paper meet, make a double or triple fold on the three open edges, and, when all three sides are folded, make a crinkly zig-zag fold along each side (*as illustrated*).

Now, heat the oil to a high temperature and quickly fry five or six parcels together for about one minute, turning over occasionally to make sure the meat is cooked on both sides. The parcels will puff up as they cook and, provided you have folded them carefully, should stay intact. Remove them from the oil and stand on kitchen paper to get rid of excess oil before serving. The paper is not edible so tear open the parcels and remove the meat to eat.

Complementary Dishes

Stir-fried Scallops (*page* 44)
Lemon Beef Soup (*page* 40)
Stir-fried Chicken with Broad Beans (*page* 72)
Peking Duck (*page* 54)

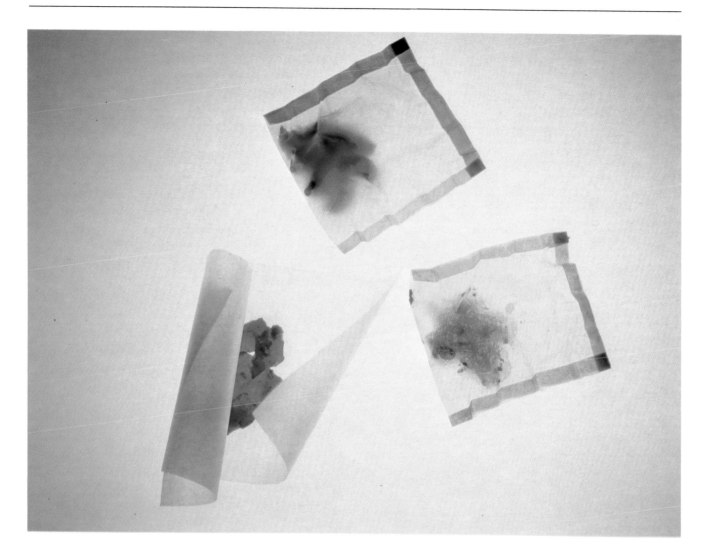

Stuffed Fillet of Sole

Makes 10 pieces

10 oz (300 g) fillet of Dover sole **or** lemon sole
2 oz (60 g) bamboo shoots
3 oz dried Chinese mushrooms
1 oz (30 g) spring onion
1 egg, beaten
3 oz (90 g) fine white breadcrumbs
salt and white pepper
1½ pints (850 ml) corn oil

Ingredients for the serving sauce

3 tablespoons (45 ml) plum sauce
½ tablespoon (7.5 ml) light-coloured soy sauce
    (*optional*)

Soak the Chinese mushrooms in boiling water, covered, for 30 minutes, remove the stems and shred finely. Place on a medium-sized plate. Cut the bamboo shoots into extremely tiny shreds (the smaller the better) and add to the plate with the shredded mushrooms.

Wash and dry the spring onions and cut into very thin slices approximately 2" (5 cm) long diagonally across. Put these on the plate with the rest of the vegetables.

Wash the fish and dry with plenty of kitchen paper. Trim the fillet of sole into approximately ⅛" (3 mm) thick slices about 2" (5 cm) wide and 3" (7.5 cm) long – like smoked salmon.

Lay a few strands of bamboo shoots, Chinese mushrooms and a few pieces of spring onion on each fillet, wrapping the fish tightly around the filling to form a roll about 1" (2.5 cm) in diameter. Repeat this process until all the slices of sole have been used up.

Dip each fillet into a bowl of beaten egg, then roll it in a bowl of seasoned breadcrumbs and put on a plate.

Heat the oil in the wok to a medium temperature. Then gently put in the fillets one at a time. Deep fry for approximately 30 seconds or until they are golden brown all over.

Remove from the wok and place on kitchen paper to absorb any excess oil before serving, perhaps with a few spring onion flowers (*page* 30) as a decoration.

Complementary Dishes

Chicken with Leeks (*page* 96)
Yam Noodles (*page* 42)
Cantonese Pork Fillet (*page* 86)

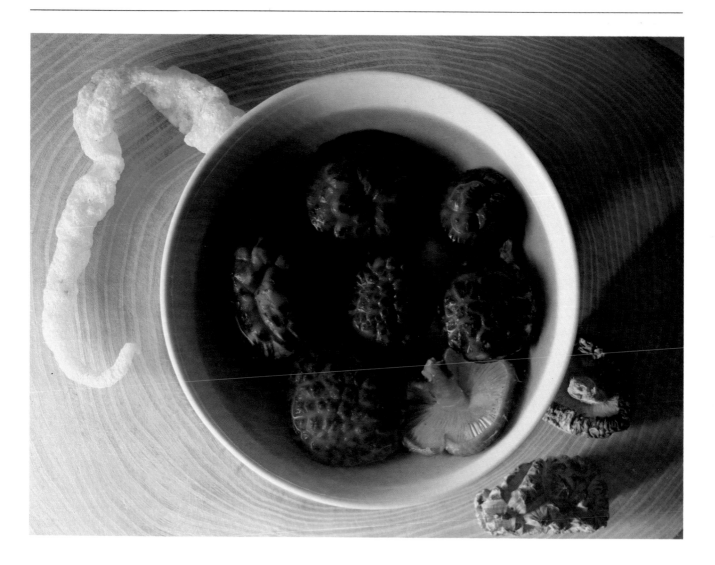

Chinese mushrooms are one of the most distinctive and versatile ingredients of Chinese cooking.

Cantonese Pork Fillet

Serves 4–6

1 lb (450 g) pork tenderloin
½ teaspoon salt
4 oz (110 ml) light-coloured soy sauce
3 oz (90 g) granulated sugar
1 teaspoon sesame paste
1 tablespoon (15 ml) sweet chilli sauce
2 teaspoons (10 ml) sesame oil
1 spring onion, chopped
2 tablespoons (30 ml) maltose **or** golden syrup
2 tablespoons (30 ml) Shaoshing wine **or** dry sherry
¼ pint (150 ml) hot water
1 tiny pinch of red colouring powder (*optional*)

Wash the pork and dry with kitchen paper and remove any skin, keeping a little of the fat (this will help to keep the meat tender and improve its texture). Then, score the surface very lightly with a knife and flatten the meat with the side of the cleaver to tenderise it. Sprinkle all over with the salt, and place the meat skewers in a deep enough dish for marinating.

Next, make the marinating sauce in a medium-size bowl. Put in the maltose or golden syrup and the hot water, then add the soy sauce, sugar, sweet chilli sauce, chopped spring onion, sesame oil, sesame paste, Shaoshing wine or sherry and the red powder. Stir well to blend all the ingredients. Pour all the sauce into the dish containing the meat, and marinate 24 hours turning frequently if not completely covered to make sure the meat is well flavoured before cooking. The, divide the meat between the skewers and drain on a rack for an hour before cooking.
Place one of the oven shelves on its highest slot and remove the rest. Place a large roasting pan in the bottom and pre-heat the oven at 475⁰F/240⁰C/Gas 9. Now hang the skewered meat from the shelf on the meat hooks and cook for 15–20 minutes.

Let the meat cool down before removing from the skewers and cutting it into thin slices across the grain. Meanwhile, heat a little of the marinating sauce, bring to the boil, and pour over the sliced meat. This is a dish that is normally prepared well in advance, since it can be served either cold or warm. It can be reheated in the oven for 5 minutes, wrapped in aluminium foil. In either case slicing is done just before serving. Do not worry if the centre of the meat is slightly pink. This is caused by the marinade. The outside should be slightly charred.

As this is quite a complicated recipe I usually prepare more than I need to make a delicious addition to fried rice or noodles at a later meal. It keeps for two or three days in a refrigerator if wrapped in foil.

Complementary Dishes

Spinach Parcel Soup (*page 102*)
Chicken with Celery (*page 98*)
Beef and Green Peppers with Noodles (*page 50*)

Small sausages, made of pork, beef, or pork liver and duck, can be kept for months. They are always cooked by steaming before they are added to a dish.

Transparent Noodles with Dried Shrimps

Serves 4–6

4 oz (120 g) transparent noodles (cellophane noodles)
2 oz (60 g) dried shrimps
2 oz (60 g) spring onion
2 oz (60 g) Chinese parsley (fresh coriander)
3 oz (90 g) Spanish onion
¼ teaspoon salt
4 oz (110 ml) chicken stock (slightly seasoned)
3 tablespoons (45 ml) corn oil
1 tablespoon (15 ml) dark-coloured soy sauce
¼ teaspoon (1.25 ml) sesame oil
a few thin slices of fresh chilli (*optional*)

Soak the transparent noodles in a bowl with cold water for 10 minutes. Drain, shake off excess water and return to the same bowl.

Soak the dried shrimps in a bowl with hot water for half an hour, drain and dry with kitchen paper before chopping into tiny pieces (this can be done with a blender or food-processor). Set aside in a bowl.

Wash the spring onion and the Chinese parsley and dry them with kitchen paper before chopping them finely with a knife, then set aside together in a bowl. Cut first the Spanish onion, and then the fresh chillis into thin slices, then place them in two separate bowls.

Heat 1 tablespoon (15 ml) of the oil in a pre-heated wok, at a medium temperature. Stir fry the Spanish onion with the salt for 25 seconds, then add the rest of the oil and the shrimps. Stir fry for a further 30 seconds before adding the noodles. After stirring a few times, add half of the stock, continue to stir fry for a few more seconds before adding the rest of the stock and the soy sauce to the noodles. Stir fry to mix and then add the spring onions, Chinese parsley and the fresh chilli (if used). Stir fry together a few more times and finally sprinkle over the sesame oil. Cook for another 2–3 seconds and the dish is ready to be served. The total cooking time should not be more than 4–5 minutes.

Complementary Dishes

Lemon Beef Soup (*page* 40)
Stir-fried Prawns with Ginger (*page* 90)
Drunken Fish (*page* 26)
Bean-Paste Chicken (*page* 46)

Stir-fried Prawns with Ginger

Serves 4–6

1 lb (450 g) uncooked Pacific **or** King Prawns – the ideal
    size is about 4″ (10 cm) long without the head
2½ tablespoons (37.5 ml) tomato sauce
5–6 thin slices fresh peeled ginger
1 large garlic clove, crushed
½ teaspoon salt
½–1 teaspoon granulated sugar
1 tablespoon (15 ml) dark-coloured soy sauce
1 tablespoon (15 ml) Shaoshing wine **or** dry sherry
2 tablespoons (30 ml) corn oil

First, trim off the legs of the prawns, wash them and dry
with plenty of kitchen paper. (The heads and shells are
left on for this recipe.) Measure the tomato sauce into a
small bowl to be used later. (You will not have time to
measure once you start to cook.)

Heat the corn oil with the garlic in a pre-heated wok at a
high temperature, extract as much juice as possible from
the garlic by pressing with a fish slice or spatula, then
discard when it begins to brown.

Then, quickly throw in the ginger and stir fry briefly
before adding the prawns and salt. Do not stir them for
1 minute then turn them over to cook for another minute
without stirring. Now, quickly pour in the tomato and
soy sauces and start to fry the prawns in order to
blend in the sauce. Add the Shaoshing wine or sherry
and the sugar, continue to cook for another minute and
they are ready to be served on a pre-heated plate. The
total cooking time is about 4–5 minutes.

Complementary Dishes

Green and White Chicken Soup (*page* 100)
Roast Beggar Chicken (*page* 20)
Beef with Black Soy Beans (*page* 64)
Traditional Fried Noodles (*page* 50)

CHINESE DELIGHTS

Steamed Grey Mullet with Lemon

Serves 4–6

1 lb 4 oz (600 g) fresh grey mullet, whole
2 tablespoons tinned salted black soy beans
1 lemon
2½ tablespoons (37.5 ml) corn oil
1 tablespoon (15 ml) light-coloured soy sauce
¾ teaspoon salt
3 pinches white pepper
1 pint (550 ml) hot water

Cut half the lemon into 12 half-slices and put them in a small bowl. Squeeze the juice from the other half into another bowl. Heat ½ tablespoon (7.5 ml) of corn oil in a small saucepan, stir fry the black soy beans for a few seconds and transfer into another small bowl with the soy sauce.

Wash and dry the fish thoroughly with plenty of the kitchen paper and then score it ½″ (1.25 cm) deep along the spine with a knife. Season it inside and out with the salt and white pepper, and place on a heat-proof shallow dish. Decorate the fish with the lemon slices and the black soy beans (*as illustrated*). Finally, pour the rest of the corn oil and the lemon juice all over the fish. Bring the hot water to the boil in a wok with a steaming rack and rest the plate with the fish on the rack. Cover the wok with a tight fitting lid in order to retain the maximum heat from the steam (it sometimes helps to place something heavy on top of the lid). Steam the fish for about 8 minutes, and then it is ready to serve.

Complementary Dishes

Paper Parcels (*page* 82)
Lamb with Green Peppers (*page* 78)
Stir-fried Chinese Cabbage (*page* 31)

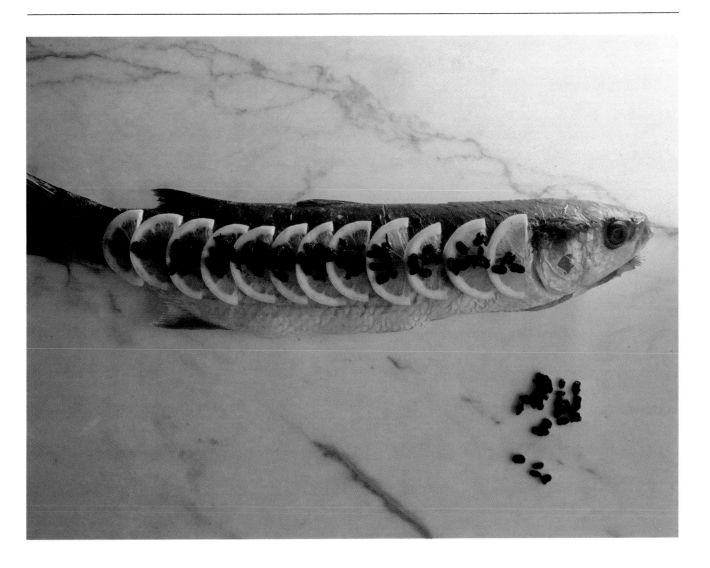

Another typical Cantonese dish.

Steamed Fresh Scallops

Serves 4–6

12 scallops (must be fresh)
8 shells
4 tablespoons (60 ml) corn oil
2 spring onions (use green part only)
2 tablespoons (30 ml) light-coloured soy sauce
1 tablespoon shredded ginger root (peeled)

Finely slice spring onions lengthwise and cut into 1″ (2.5 cm) strips. Divide the ginger and onions into two equal portions and mix together and place in two of the shells. Put to one side. Wash and dry the scallops, retaining the roes. Bring the water to the boil in a wok. Place two scallops in each of the remaining shells and steam on a large rack for approximately 6 minutes. Before serving, heat the oil and soy sauce in a small saucepan and pour over the two shells containing the ginger and spring onions. Serve hot. Dip the scallops into the sauce.

Complementary Dishes

Wun-Tun Soup (*page 34*)
Braised Leg of Pork (*page 36*)
Stir-fried Chicken with Broad Beans (*page 72*)

Chicken with Leeks

Serves 4–6

2½–3 lb (1.25 kg–1.5 kg) fresh chicken
1 lb (450 g) fresh young leeks
4 tablespoons (60 ml) corn oil
1½ teaspoons salt
3 pinches of white pepper
2 teaspoons (10 ml) light-coloured soy sauce
½–¾ pint (275–425 ml) stock (highly seasoned)
2 teaspoons (10 ml) granulated sugar
2 tablespoons (30 ml) Shaoshing wine or dry sherry
2 slices of fresh ginger
2 cloves of crushed garlic
½–1 teaspoon cornflour mixed with 1 tablespoon
    (15 ml) cold water

Split the leeks in half lengthwise and wash them thoroughly with cold water. Shake off excess water before cutting them diagonally into ¼ inch (6 mm) thick slices, place them in a bowl and leave until later.

Wash and dry the chicken thoroughly. Then, using a sharp cleaver, chop along the backbone and split the chicken open. Remove any fat around the tail end and season all over with salt and pepper.

Heat 2 tablespoons (30 ml) of corn oil at a high temperature for a few seconds, in a pre-heated frying pan with the garlic and the ginger, but before they are brown, gently put in the chicken with the skin side down. Let the skin brown lightly before carefully turning the chicken over to cook on the other side. It is very important to handle it carefully so as not to tear the skin, which would spoil the appearance.

And now for the braising. Transfer the contents of the frying pan to a sandpot (or a saucepan). Cook over medium heat, add stock, soy sauce, Shaoshing wine and sugar, bring to the boil, then simmer on a low heat until the chicken is very tender to touch with the point of a fork. This will take approximately 1½ hours. Be careful not to overcook as it might become impossible to transfer the chicken to a serving dish without it breaking up.

Before serving, thicken the sauce with the cornflour mixture and pour over the chicken.

Finally, heat 2 tablespoons (30 ml) of corn oil with ½ teaspoon salt and stir fry the leeks for about ten minutes (in the same frying pan used already to fry the chicken). It may be necessary to turn down the heat a little to avoid scorching them. When cooked, spread the leeks evenly around the chicken and serve.

The chicken can be cooked in advance, but do not cook the leeks until it is time to serve as they must remain fresh green in colour.

Complementary Dishes

Spicy Rolls (*page 68*)
Cantonese Pork Fillet (*page 86*)
Beef with Black Soy Beans (*page 64*)

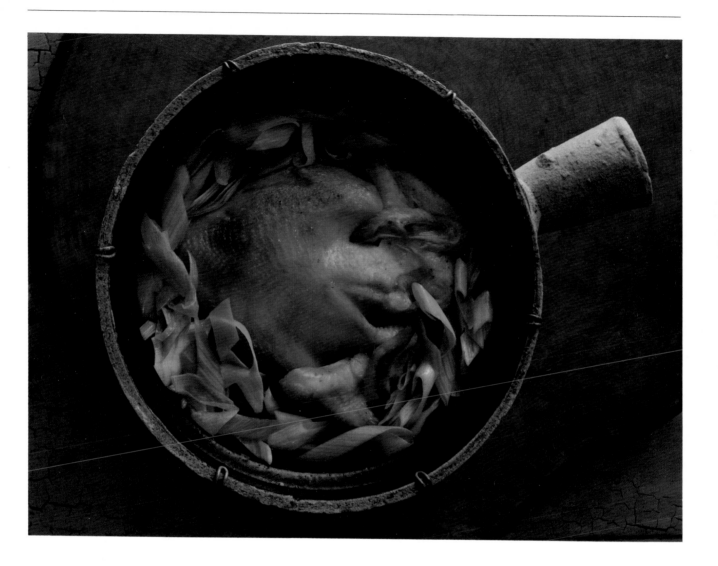

Chicken with Celery

Serves 4–6

1 lb (450 g) breast of chicken off the bone
4 stalks celery (green)
1 teaspoon salt
5 tablespoons (75 ml) corn oil
2 teaspoons granulated sugar
pinch of white pepper
1 teaspoon cornflour
1 tablespoon salt

Shred the chicken as shown on page 41. Marinate with salt, pepper, cornflour, sugar and half the tablespoon (15 ml) oil.

Slice the celery diagonally ⅛″ (3 mm) thick, add a pinch of salt and stir fry in 2 tablespoons (30 ml) oil over low to medium heat for about 1½ minutes. Place it in a bowl.

Heat the remaining oil to medium hot, add the shredded chicken and quickly stir fry for 2 minutes. Add one tablespoon (15 ml) of water and the cooked celery and remaining sugar and fry for a further 30 seconds at the most.

Complementary Dishes

Spare Ribs (*page* 106)
Paper Parcels (*page* 82)
Smoked Halibut (*page* 104)

Green and White Chicken Soup

Serves 4–6

4 oz (120 g) breast of chicken off the bone
5 oz (150 g) fresh spinach
6 egg whites
1/3 teaspoon salt
9 teaspoons cornflour
3 pinches white pepper
4 tablespoons (60 ml) water

Ingredients for the stock

3 lb (1.5 kg) chicken carcass pieces for making soup
4 pints (2.25 litres) water
2 pinches white pepper

Complementary Dishes

Drunken Fish (*page 26*)
Stir-fried Mangetout and Chinese Sausages (*page 60*)
Roast Beggar Chicken (*page 20*)
Fried Rice (*page 52*)

To make the stock

Bring the water to the boil, then put in the carcass and cook for 5 minutes at a high temperature. Skim off any impurities. Turn down the heat and simmer for about 1 1/2 hours. The stock should now be reduced to about 3 pints (1.7 litres). Remove the pieces of chicken before seasoning with salt and pepper. Pour the stock through a very fine sieve or a piece of cheesecloth to remove any remaining small particles.

Wash the chicken breast and dry with kitchen paper and mince it finely. Place the minced chicken in a bowl, season with 1/3 teaspoon of salt, 1/4 teaspoon of cornflour, and the pepper. Mix and leave on one side. Wash the spinach and dry as thoroughly as possible with plenty of kitchen paper, then chop the leaves finely by hand or in a food-processor. Set the chopped leaves aside in a bowl.

To make the white soup

Pour 1 pint (550 ml) of cold chicken stock into a saucepan, empty in the bowl of minced chicken. Bring slowly to the boil stirring rapidly with a fork or a small wire into the stock. Stir rapidly with a fork or a small wire whisk until all the meat has separated into tiny pieces, then turn the heat to medium temperature, add a mixture of 3 teaspoons of cornflour and 1 tablespoon (15 ml) of cold water. Keep stirring and when the soup begins to thicken, pour in two of the egg whites. It is important to stir rapidly in a clockwise direction, in order to transform the egg white into a mass of fine shreds. Turn down the heat as soon as the egg white has begun to solidify, do not overcook it, and keep the soup in a warm place while you continue with the rest of the recipe.

To make the green soup

Bring 1 1/2 pints (850 ml) chicken stock to just under boiling point and thicken with 6 teaspoons of cornflour mixed with 2 tablespoons (30 ml) of cold water. Then, pour in the four remaining egg whites and proceed exactly as you did with the white chicken soup (above). Remember to keep the temperature low at all times.

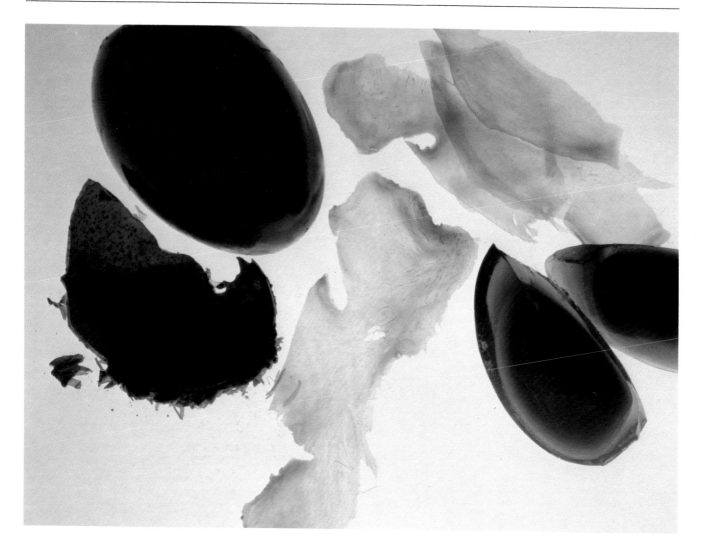

The most famous Chinese delicacy, Thousand Year Eggs are duck eggs 'pickled' by wrapping them in a lime and straw compost.

When the egg white has started to set, mix the chopped spinach with the soup. Turn up the heat a little and bring to just below boiling point. Now, heat the white soup to just below boiling point, then place a small round buttomless ring or cake tin (or any interestingly shaped mould with an open base) at the bottom of a pre-warmed soup tureen and, holding one saucepan in each hand, gently pour the green and white soups to the same depth, using the ring or mould to keep the colours separate by pouring one inside and the other outside. (I allow a bigger area for the green soup.) Finally, gently lift the mould out of the soup and you will have achieved an exotic looking and extremely tasty soup.

Spinach Parcel Soup

Serves 4–6

7 oz (200 g) fillet of monkfish **or** turbot **or** cod steak
¼ teaspoon salt
2 pinches white pepper
a little chopped spring onion
¾ lb (350 g) spinach

Ingredients for the stock

3 lb (1.5 kg) chicken carcass pieces
4 pints (2.25 litres) water
2 teaspoons salt
2 pinches white pepper
1 thin slice peeled ginger

First make the stock following the method given in the recipe for Green and White Chicken Soup (*page* 100). Next, wash the fish and dry with kitchen paper. Cut into slices about ¼″ (6 mm) thick, 2″ (5 cm) by 1″ (2.5 cm) in size. Mix with ¼ teaspoon each of salt and white pepper in a bowl and set aside.

Wash the spinach (using leaves without any splits or holes) and remove all the stems. Bring a saucepan of slightly salted water to the boil and blanch the spinach for a couple of seconds with the heat turned off. Strain and dry the leaves individually. Pick out each leaf, lay it flat on a wooden board, place one or two pieces of the fish in one corner, fold in the other three corners. Then roll up the fish in the spinach, making a small neat parcel about 2½″ long by 1″ wide (6 cm by 2.5 cm). If the leaves are not large enough to wrap the fish use two leaves together. Repeat until all the slices of fish have been wrapped in the same way.

Place the spinach parcels into a shallow saucepan. Gently pour in half of the hot chicken stock (enough just to cover the parcels) and cook for approximately 5–6 minutes on a medium heat. Then add the rest of the hot stock.

Sprinkle with a little chopped spring onion and it is ready to be served.

Complementary Dishes

Sliced Pork with Wooden Ears (*page* 24)
Chicken with Leeks (*page* 96)
Stir-fried Prawns with Ginger (*page* 90)
Fresh Steamed Scallops (*page* 94)

The fire pot provides a lazy and luxurious way of eating the many traditional Chinese dishes served in stock. The glowing charcoal in the middle keeps the liquid hot enough to cook further ingredients – meat, fish, poultry and vegetables – to individual taste at the table.

Smoked Halibut

Serves 4–6

1 lb (450 g) fresh halibut (with the skin intact)
2–3 tablespoons (30–45 ml) dark-coloured soy sauce
1–2 teaspoons granulated sugar
2 tablespoons chopped spring onion
1 tablespoon finely chopped fresh ginger
3 tablespoons (45 ml) Shaoshing wine **or** dry sherry
½ teaspoon cornflour mixed with
   1 teaspoon (15 ml) cold water
2 teaspoons Chinese tea leaves
3 pinches of white pepper
2 complete star anise (or the equivalent in small pieces)
1½ pints (850 ml) corn oil

The slices of fish should not be more than ½″ (1.25 cm) thick and you should be able to get three small-medium size steaks from a piece of fish weighing 1 lb (450 g).

Wash the steaks and dry them well with plenty of kitchen paper. Crush the chopped ginger with the Shaoshing wine or sherry and star anise and allow to stand for 15 minutes. Then, strain over a bowl, pressing down with a spoon to extract as much liquid as possible. Mix this ginger-flavoured wine with the soy sauce, spring onion and the pepper in a large bowl. Put in the fish and allow to stand for 2 hours, turning the fish over every half hour, making sure it is well marinated on both sides.

Heat the oil in a wok at a high temperature (it will take approximately 5 minutes), and deep fry the fish, keeping the marinade aside. Gently remove the fish from the oil and rest on some kitchen paper to absorb excess oil before placing it on a cake-rack in a warm place. Empty out all the oil and clean and dry the wok before placing the tea in it. Turn the heat to high. Once the tea begins to smoke, insert the rack (with the fish slices) in the middle of the wok, cover with a wok lid, and smoke for about 1 minute. Remove and place on a pre-heated serving plate and keep warm. Meanwhile, heat the marinade, thicken with the cornflour and cold water mixture. When you have a translucent thickish sauce pour over the fish and serve.

This is a Shanghai dish. The recipe can be used for other firm-fleshed white fish.

Complementary Dishes

Beef with Black Soy Beans (*page 64*)
Chicken with Celery (*page 98*)
Stuffed Aubergines (*page 108*)
Plain Boiled Rice (*page 27*)

Fish and seafood are very important in the diet of the Chinese people, as half of the country is surrounded by sea and there are many great rivers. The photograph shows small fish salted and dried in the sun. These will be steamed with a few drops of oil and thin shreds of ginger root before serving.

Spare Ribs

Serves 4–6

2½ lb (1.25 kg) long spare ribs
2 slices fresh peeled ginger
2 cloves garlic, crushed
⅓ pint (200 ml) hot water
3 tablespoons (45 ml) corn oil

Marinating ingredients

2 tablespoons (30 ml) tomato sauce
1 tablespoon (15 ml) sweet chilli sauce
2 teaspoons (10 ml) Worcestershire sauce
3 tablespoons (45 ml) dark-coloured soy sauce
3 tablespoons (45 ml) Shaoshing wine **or** dry sherry
½ teaspoon sesame oil
1 oz (30 g) spring onion, chopped
2 teaspoons (10 ml) cornflour
1–1½ tablespoons (15–22.5 ml) golden syrup
¼–½ teaspoon salt
¼ teaspoon five spice powder
3 pinches of white pepper

In a muslin bag

1½ tablespoons (22.5 ml) Szechuan peppercorns
2 complete star anise (or the equivalent in small pieces)

Complementary Dishes

Spinach Parcel Soup (*page* 102)
Chicken with Pickled Vegetables (*page* 66)
Boiled Noodles (*page* 62)

Cut the spare ribs into separate pieces and trim off any excess fat. Place them in a big mixing bowl and marinate with all the marinating ingredients for two hours. Remember to turn them a few times to make sure each rib is well covered with the marinade.

Heat the oil in a pre-heated wok or saucepan at a high temperature, add the ginger and the garlic to flavour the oil. Empty the ribs and the marinade into the wok and cook for ten minutes, stirring constantly to prevent the ribs from sticking to the bottom of the pan. Then add the hot water and bring to the boil. Turn down the heat to low and simmer for about 50 minutes. The sauce should then be thickened and reduced to just less than half the original amount, and the dish is ready for serving.
For a crispier result remove the ribs from the sauce just before serving and deep fry in oil for a couple of minutes.

Also in the photograph are Star Anise and Szechuan Peppercorns.

Stuffed Aubergines

Serves 4–6

6 oz (180 g) fresh pork, with a little fat
10 oz (300 g) small fresh aubergine. 2″ (5 cm) in diameter
  is a perfect size
½ egg, beaten
1½ (22.5 ml) tablespoons light-coloured soy sauce
2 tablespoons finely chopped spring onion
1½ teaspoon granulated sugar
1 teaspoon cornflour
4 tablespoons (60 ml) corn oil
2 pinches white pepper
2 slices fresh peeled ginger
2 cloves garlic, crushed
½ teaspoon (2.5 ml) sesame oil (*optional*)
2 oz (46 ml) hot water or stock if available
2 oz (60 g) plain flour

Slice the aubergine crosswise about ⅛″ (3 mm) thick, but on every second cut go only three quarters of the way through to form hinged 'oyster shells'. Repeat until you have twelve pairs and leave them all in a bowl to sweat with a little salt for half an hour. Then rinse them with cold water and dry with plenty of kitchen paper. Next, mince the pork with a cleaver (*see page* 19), mix in the egg and half of the cornflour, together with the tablespoons soy sauce and half of the sugar. Stir vigorously until the egg is well blended with the meat – this will take a few seconds. Then add 1 each 'oyster shell' with the meat stuffing to form a sandwich, making it neat around the edge. Dust each stuffed aubergine all over with flour and place them on a plate.

Mix the water (or stock) with the rest of the cornflour, to be used later. Heat 2 tablespoons (30 ml) of oil in a pre-heated wok at a high temperature, flavoured with the garlic and the ginger, removing the pieces once the flavour has been absorbed into the oil. Then quickly put in the aubergines, and fry until golden brown on both sides. After cooking for 3 – 4 minutes, pour in the rest of the oil around the sides of the wok above the aubergines, in order to distribute it evenly. The total cooking time is about 7 – 8 minutes.

Now, add the cornflour mixture to the aubergines and cook until the sauce thickens. Sprinkle with sesame oil and the remaining spring onions before serving.

This dish can be made ahead of time, and only needs warming up before serving.

Complementary Dishes

Wun-Tun Soup with Watercress (*page* 34)
Chicken with Pickled Vegetables (*page* 66)
Steamed Trout (*page* 80)
Plain Boiled Rice (*page* 27)

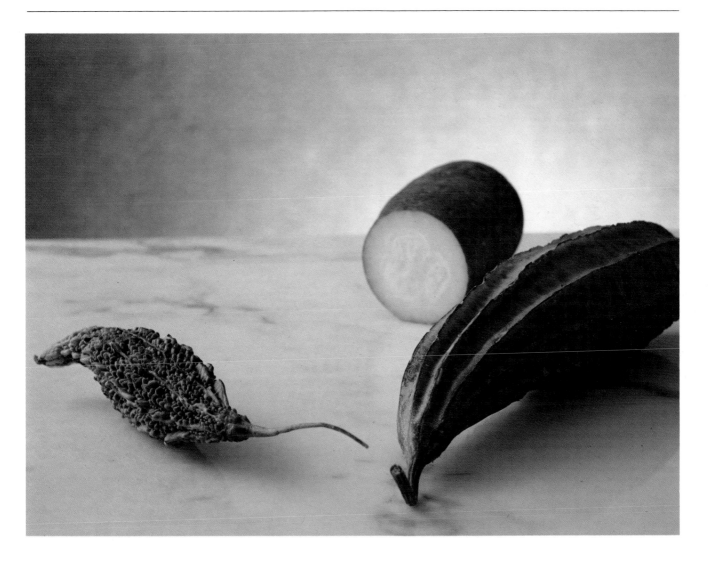

In Chinese cooking, vegetables are considered as important as the 'main' ingredient (meat, poultry, fish), especially in stir-fry cooking.

Chilled Snow Ears with Kiwi Fruit

Serves 4–6

1 oz (30 g) snow ears (white tree fungus)
1½ pints (850 ml) water
5–6 oz (150–180 g) Chinese crystal sugar or
  granulated sugar
5 fresh Kiwi fruit

Soak the snow ears in a big bowl of cold water for approximately 25 minutes or until they have become almost white in colour and have doubled in size. Empty the contents of the bowl into a sink full of cold water and wash the snow ears carefully. Repeat a few times with fresh water until there is no trace of any impurities or grit. Then trim off any remaining yellow hard pieces. Place the snow ears in a colander to drain.

Boil the water with the sugar for 15 minutes without a lid. The liquid will reduce by about one third. Turn off the heat, add the snow ears and stir well in the syrup for a few minutes before pouring into a shallow serving dish to cool.

Decorate with peeled and thinly sliced Kiwi fruit arranged in a ring around the edge of the dish, or in any other imaginative way, and place the dish in the refrigerator until you are ready to serve.

This dessert can be served hot equally well, and it is not necessary to serve it with fruit.

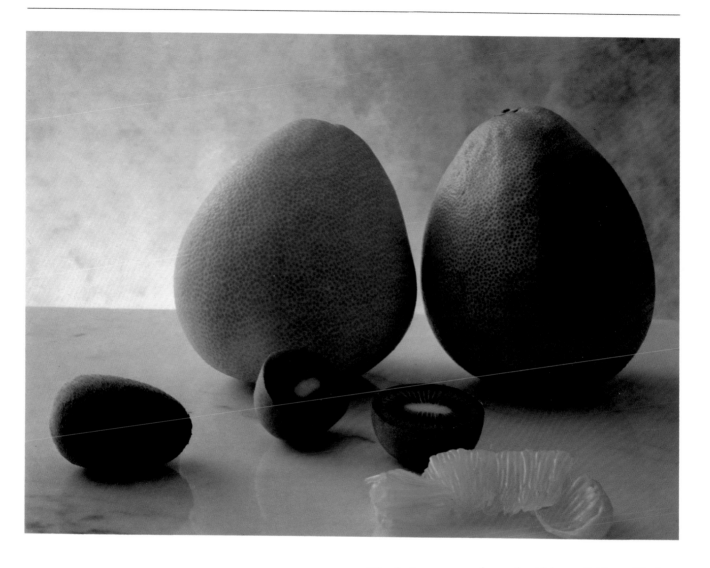

The fruit now popular and widely available as Kiwi Fruit used to be known as Chinese Gooseberry. Also in the photograph are Pomelo, twice the size of grapefruit but much sweeter.

INGREDIENTS

It is true to say that a simple Chinese meal can be cooked with whatever you have in the cupboard, as long as a bottle of soy sauce, garlic and fresh ginger are available. But in order to cook any of the wide selection of classic dishes, it is essential to obtain the true Chinese ingredients for which there are no substitutes. Nowadays, most of these ingredients are dried, canned or preserved, and can be stored indefinitely. This is a great advantage, which should enable you to build up a reasonable selection. In the following pages, I have prepared an index of special ingredients as used in the recipes.

SOY SAUCE

Description: There are basically two main types of this sauce: one light and thin (young), one dark and heavier (old). Both are made of soy beans, wheat, salt and sugar, fermented with yeast. They can be purchased either in tins or in glass or plastic bottles.

Storage: Once a tin is opened, the contents should be transferred to a jar or bottle.

Available from: Chinese shops, delicatessens or supermarkets.

BAMBOO SHOOTS

Description: This is a very widely used vegetable in Chinese cooking, which is found only in tins outside the Far East. The fibrous cream-coloured stems are usually in chunks, approximately 3" (7.5 cm) to 4" (10 cm) long and can be cut in various ways.

Storage: Once the tin is opened, the water should be changed daily in order to keep it fresh, and the container kept in the refrigerator.

Available from: Chinese shops, delicatessens and some supermarkets.

DRIED BAMBOO LEAF

Description: This is the leaf of a bamboo plant which has been dried in the sun. It is used to wrap food for cooking.

It has a very distinctive but subtle flavour, and is always sold in a bundle.

Preparation:

Bamboo leaf must be soaked in cold water for many hours (or overnight) until it is flexible to work with It needs careful handling to prevent it from splitting.

Storage:

Can be kept in its dry state indefinitely.

Available from:

Chinese shops only.

BITTER MELON

Description:

The texture and colour of this vegetable is not unlike that of the green pepper, except that it has a lumpy, uneven surface with an unusual bitter taste. It can be used, cut in pieces, for stir-fried, braised or stewed dishes.

Storage:

Can be kept in the refrigerator for up to two weeks.

Available from:

Chinese, Indian and Thai shops.

BLACK SOY BEANS

Description:

These are salty, spicy black beans which have been fermented. Either dried or tinned varieties are available. They are never eaten alone, but are used in Chinese cooking because of their special flavour.

Preparation:

Rinse the dried version with warm water before cooking in order to get rid of excess salt.

Storage:

Dried beans can be kept in a container indefinitely at room temperature. Once the tinned variety is opened, it must then be transferred into a jar and kept in the refrigerator.

Available from:

Chinese shops only.

CHINESE CABBAGE (CHINESE LEAF)

Description:

This vegetable can be found in various sizes and colours. Sometimes it can be a very pale yellow, almost white, or it can have pale green leaves and a white stem. Both have the same flavour and are as popular as the bean sprout in Chinese cooking. It can be eaten when crisp or softened after longer cooking, depending on the recipe.

Storage:

Can be kept in a plastic bag in the vegetable compartment of the refrigerator for 2 – 3 weeks.

Available from:

Chinese shops, some vegetable shops and most supermarkets.

CHINESE MUSHROOMS

Description:

These black edible fungi are one of the most distinctive and versatile ingredients for Chinese cooking. The quality is judged by the thickness – the thicker the better. They can be cooked with or without other ingredients and have a chewy texture

Preparation:

Soak in boiled water for at least half an hour, or until they are soft to touch. Always cover when soaking. Remove the stems and any pieces which have not softened. The soaking water can sometimes be used, strained, to flavour a sauce or stew.

Storage:

In an air-tight container. They cannot be kept once they have been soaked.

Available from:

Chinese shops only.

CHINESE PARSLEY (FRESH CORIANDER OR CILANTRO)

Description:

This has a much stronger flavour than the ordinary parsley and is very often used with chopped spring onion for garnishing in Chinese cooking, but also as a vegetable.

Storage:

As long as it remains dry, it can be kept in a plastic bag in the refrigerator, for up to ten days. It can also be frozen successfully in plastic bags or glass jars.

Available from:

Chinese, Indian, Greek or Cypriot grocery shops.

CHINESE SAUSAGES

Description:

There are three different kinds of these cured sausages: pork, beef, and pork liver and duck. The texture and appearance is very similar to that of small-size salami, but they have a slightly sweet taste

Preparation:

They must be cooked by steaming before adding to other ingredients or serving alone.

Storage:

Can be kept in a plastic bag in the refrigerator for a few months.

Available from:

Chinese shops only.

CHINESE SUGAR

Description:

There are at least two types of Chinese sugar, a pale yellow clear crystal, or a brown coloured slab; both are natural, or unrefined

Storage:

Can be kept in an air-tight jar or tin indefinitely.

Available from:

Chinese shops only.

DRIED PEEL

Description:

This is dried orange, tangerine, lemon or grapefruit peel, sold together in one package or individually. When added to cooking, dried peel gives a distinctive tangy flavour.

Preparation:	Must be soaked in warm water for at least half an hour before cooking.
Storage:	They should be kept in an air-tight jar.
Available from:	Chinese shops only.

DRIED SHRIMPS

Description:	These are small and orange coloured, and are available in different qualities. They have been salted and dried in the sun and have a distinctive fishy smell and taste. The bigger they are, the better the quality.
Preparation:	They must be soaked in lukewarm water for at least half an hour, then drained and dried on kitchen paper.
Storage:	They can be kept in the dry state in an air-tight container indefinitely.
Available from:	Chinese shops only.

FISH INTESTINES

Description:	These dried intestines are off-white in colour and have an irregular tubular shape. They are eaten rather for their texture than their taste.
Preparation:	Soak in warm water for half an hour, or until soft, before cooking.
Storage:	Can be kept in the dry state in a plastic bag or air-tight container at room temperature indefinitely.
Available from:	Chinese shops only.

FIVE SPICE POWDER

Description:	This medium brown coloured, heavily scented

powder can be bought ready made in a package or it can be blended at home, using a pestle and mortar or a coffee-mill. It consists of star anise, flower peppercorn, clove, Chinese cinnamon and fennel seed. It is sometimes called five-fragrance or five-scented powder.

Storage:

In an airtight glass jar or tin.

Available from:

Chinese shops only.

FLOWER (SZECHUAN) PEPPERCORNS

Description:

This is a tiny, round, reddish brown spice with a very fragrant smell. It can be used ground or whole. It is often used with star anise, especially for red-stewed dishes.

Storage:

Best kept in an air-tight jar.

Available from:

Chinese shops or fresh herb and spice shops.

GLUTINOUS RICE

Description:

This rice is shorter and rounder than the average long-grain rice and a little more opaque in colour. It can be used in both savoury and sweet dishes and has a very sticky texture once cooked.

Preparation:

Must be rinsed with cold water a few times before cooking.

Storage:

Can be kept in the same way as any other grain.

Available from:

Chinese shops only.

GLUTINOUS RICE FLOUR

Description:

This is a very fine ground flour made from glutinous rice. It is often used with savoury as well as sweet fillings. Once it is cooked, it has an extremely chewy, soft texture.

Storage: Can be kept in the same way as any other flour.

Available from: Chinese shops only.

HOI SIN SAUCE

Description: This thick dark brown sauce can be made from soy sauce, sugar, salt, garlic, red beans, and soy bean flour in a blender, or it can be bought ready-made in a tin or jar. It is used both in cooking and in serving.

Storage: Can be kept at room temperature indefinitely.

Available from: Chinese shops only.

PICKLED CABBAGE

Description: These crisp, thin stem pieces of vegetables, approximately 1″ (2.5 cm) long and dull green, are preserved in brine and have a crisp texture. Pickled cabbage can only be bought in a tin.

Storage: Once the tin is opened, the cabbage must be transferred to an airtight jar, and can be kept in the refrigerator for a few days.

Preparation: Before cooking, the cabbage must be rinsed in cold water, then squeezed by hand to remove excess water and cut to the appropriate size.

Available from: Chinese shops only. A good brand is Ma Ling.

PLUM SAUCE

Description: This is made of yellow plums, sugar, water, salt, garlic and chilli cooked down into a sweet, spicy thick sauce, or it can be bought in glass bottles or jars. It can be used in cooking as well as serving.

Storage: Can be kept in cupboard indefinitely.

Available from: Chinese shops.

SATÉ SAUCE

Description:

This is a brown thick sauce made from soy sauce, sugar, peanut oil, spices, salt and chilli, originating from Malaya. It has a very distinct hot, nutty flavour. Used essentially as a table sauce, but can also be used as flavouring for cooking. It is available in jars only. It can be made at home and recipes will be found in Thai and other South-east Asian cookery books.

Storage:

Can be kept indefinitely.

Available from:

Chinese shops and Malaysian or Thai shops.

SESAME SEEDS

Description:

These seeds come in two colours, black and white, and both have exactly the same flavour. They can be used in cooking as well as garnishing and the choice of colour is entirely personal.

Storage:

Can be kept in an air-tight container indefinitely.

Available from:

Chinese shops, health-food shops and most Indian shops.

SESAME OIL

Description:

This oil is the extract of the white roasted sesame seed. It has a strong distinct nutty flavour and a deep golden colour with a thickish texture. It is never used in cooking, but for seasoning only. There is also a cheaper version of this oil, which is made of vegetable oil with sesame flavouring. Both are obtainable only in bottles.

Storage:

Can be kept at room temperature indefinitely.

Available from:

Chinese and Indian shops and health-food shops.

SHAOSHING WINE

Description: This is a drinking wine distilled from glutinous rice, light brown in colour, and the flavour – rather like a medium sherry – is slightly different from the Japanese Saké (rice wine).

Storage: Can be kept at room temperature indefinitely.

Available from: Chinese shops only.

SILVER EARS

Description: A white edible dried fungus, which has little or no taste but has a delicate texture and is served only as a dessert.

Preparation: Soak in cold water for an hour until swollen.

Storage: In the dry state may be kept indefinitely in an air-tight jar.

Available from: Chinese shops only.

SNOW PEAS (MANGETOUT PEAS)

Description: The French name for these peas is 'Mangetout' because the young vegetable can be eaten complete' with pod. It is therefore important when selecting them to choose the small thin ones, as the thicker they are, the older and tougher they become.

Preparation: Pull off the stalk and attached strings and do likewise with the tail.

Storage: Can be kept in the vegetable compartment of the refrigerator for up to a week.

Available from: Chinese shops, vegetable shops and most supermarkets.

STAR ANISE

Description: This is a highly scented star-shaped spice, dark brown in colour, and is widely used in red-stewing recipes.

Storage: Must be kept in an air-tight jar to preserve its aroma.

Available from: Chinese and Indian shops.

SZECHUAN PASTE

Ingredients: The basic ingredients are hot chilli, peppers, salt, sugar, garlic, soy beans and oil. It is extremely hot and either a little is added during the cooking process or a little dish is served separately on the table. Available only in jars.

Storage: Can be kept indefinitely at room temperature.

Available from: Chinese shops only.

WATER CHESTNUTS

Description: Fresh water chestnuts have white flesh with a black-coloured skin. They have a crisp texture with a sweet taste. Unfortunately, fresh water chestnuts can only be bought occasionally from Chinese grocery stores, the alternative being the canned ones, which I personally feel are no substitute.

Preparation: Fresh water chestnuts must be washed thoroughly, then the black skin peeled off.

Storage: Can be kept at room temperature for up to two weeks.

Available from: Chinese shops only.

blending soya beans, wheat flour, sugar and soy sauce to a thick medium-brown paste. It can also be purchased in a tin. For extra flavour, this sauce is added at the last minute of cooking.

Storage:

Once the tin is opened, the contents must be transferred to a jar, and it can then be kept in the refrigerator indefinitely.

Available from:

Chinese shops only.

WOODEN EARS

Description:

This edible black fungus is of the same family as Tree and Cloud Ears, but comes in different sizes. Unlike the Chinese Mushroom (also an edible fungus) which has a chewy texture, they are crispy to eat.

Preparation:

Soak in warm water for at least half an hour, then rinse well to get rid of any grit.

Storage:

Can be kept in a plastic bag or an air-tight container.

Available from:

Chinese shops only.

TECHNIQUES

One of the distinctive things about Chinese food is the way most of the ingredients are pre-cut into small bite-sized pieces before being cooked. As the way this is performed plays a large part in both presentation and texture, I have devoted this section to the various methods of cutting, which are constantly referred to in the recipes. Traditionally, this is carried out with a cleaver, but the same result can be achieved with a very sharp kitchen knife.

Slicing

The cutting action is vertical and the meat or vegetables should be held firmly with your free hand. The knife hand is used to regulate the thickness of the cut, both hand and knife being moved simultaneously across the ingredient as each slice is made. The thickness of the cut is regulated by the extent of each move.

A useful tip, when the ingredient becomes too small to hold, is to lay the remaining piece flat and slice horizontally. Long vegetables such as French beans, asparagus and spring onions should be cut diagonally to improve the appearance when served.

Shredding and dicing are really an extension of the slicing technique. With all three, you endeavour to keep the size of the pieces as regular as possible.

Shredding

Having sliced the ingredients, they are then laid neatly on top of each other and the procedure repeated, turning the slices into strips.

Dicing

This is a continuation of the previous two processes but the slicing and shredding should be carried out to produce strips of the same thickness and depth as you want the finished dice to be. The strips are then cut for a third time, across the length. The size of the final pieces can vary according to the dish, and this is explained more fully in individual recipes.

Mincing

Although it might seem tedious to mince one's own meat or vegetables by hand, it is essential in Chinese cooking, as a machine tends to spoil the texture of the ingredients. First follow the slicing and shredding procedure, to produce coarse strips approximately ¼″ (6 mm) thick. Then, using the cleaver, chop the ingredients at random, until they form an irregular mince. In order to ensure that the pieces are minced thoroughly, it will be necessary to turn the mass once or twice during chopping.

Scoring

This is used when cooking a whole fish or large piece of meat and entails slicing the surface diagonally with a series of parallel cuts to a depth of approximately ¼″ (6 mm) – 1″ (2.5 cm). The purpose of scoring is two-fold, first to reduce cooking time by exposing more of the flesh to the heat and secondly to tenderise it as in the case of squid or kidneys. In the latter case, a further series of cuts are added on the opposite diagonal to form a criss-cross pattern, in order to break down the surface. Apart from the practical reason I mentioned, scoring has a further advantage of being very decorative on the finished dish.

COOKING METHODS

Some of the methods might seem intriguing at first sight but the few definitions listed here are really quite obvious.

Stir Frying

This is the uniquely Chinese way of cooking.

Ingredients are always first cut into thin or small pieces and cooked very quickly with constant stirring. The food is ready after literally only a minute or two at a high temperature, but if it appears to be browning too much or too soon then the heat must be turned down, or the appearance will be spoiled. Food cooked in this way remains very fresh and crispy, especially green vegetables, and produces a contrast of colour and texture with the meat. The recipes in this book are cooked in a wok resting on a wok ring. Cooking without the ring gives more intense heat, but can be tricky for beginners.

Steaming

This is a complete contrast to the stir-fry method of cooking. Once the food is prepared there is no work to be done during the actual cooking. The food is placed in a bamboo steamer, or on a plate or dish rested on a steaming rack in the wok, which is filled with boiling water to just beneath the level of the rack or bamboo steamer, and steamed (with the wok lid on, if you are not using the bamboo steamer) at a constant high temperature until cooked. For this method, all the ingredients must be extremely fresh. The steam will bring out the natural and simple flavour of the food, which requires a relatively short cooking time – for example, a whole sea bass weighing over 3 lbs (over 1.3 kg) only needs 15–20 minutes. It is very important not to overcook any food, or you will spoil the fresh, delicate texture. For any dish needing more than 10 minutes of cooking time, you should check occasionally whether there is enough water in the wok.

Braising

This method is similar to methods used in western cooking. The raw ingredients are nearly always pre-fried first over high heat, in order to seal the meat, keep the juices in and flavour the skin, as well as give a nicer colour to the meat. It is much better to cook for a longer time over very low heat than to try to speed things up by raising the temperature. When it is cooked the meat should be extremely tender.

This is a good method for a dinner party, served among other last-minute dishes, since it can be cooked well in advance and reheated just before serving.

Deep Frying

The food is cooked in very hot oil over a high temperature, exactly like deep-frying anywhere in the world. It is important to have enough oil in the wok, approximately 1–1½ pints (550–850 ml) for an average sized wok, or a little more than half the depth of an ordinary deep-frying pan. It is also important to make sure that the oil is at the right temperature for frying. This can be assured by first testing one piece of food before cooking the rest – the oil must sizzle at once. The method of cooking takes only a short time, especially since most of the Chinese deep-fried recipes call for small portions. In fact even a whole 'crispy duck' would be steamed first, to cook and tenderise the meat, before frying to give the skin a crispy texture. After deep-frying, all food must be drained well to remove any trace of oil, in order that it should taste crisp and fresh. I use corn oil, which has less taste than some other kinds of oil.

Smoking

This is a final touch to some dishes and is common to all regional varieties of Chinese cooking. Most of the ingredients – fish, meat or fowl – would have been cooked already and are then smoked to add a distinctive taste and aroma. This is achieved simply by arranging the cooked ingredients on a rack over 2 tablespoons of dry tea in a covered wok, and placing it over high temperature. It takes only 1 or 2 minutes, depending on the size of the pieces, to produce a very impressive and extraordinary result – dishes such as the famous Cantonese 'Smoked Quail' (*page* 30) or the Shanghainese 'Smoked Fish' (*page* 104) are good examples.

Red Stewing

This method of stewing is very similar to ordinary braising but always gives a deep red appearance to the dish. This is the end result of long cooking with dark-coloured soy sauce and many spices, especially comforting during the winter season, as it makes a very tasty and heart-warming dish. This is suitable for many different types of meat and is also an amazing way of cooking fresh soy-bean curd which is a very popular Chinese dish. A good example of this cooking is Braised Leg of Pork (*page* 36).

Roasting

This particular method is less often used than other methods in Chinese cooking. But there is the famous Cantonese 'Sin Mai' which is a selection of roasted duck, fillet of pork and pork belly cooked to a deep red colour.

This type of roasted meat would be sliced thin, or chopped (in the case of duck) before being served cold, accompanied by other dishes. It is a speciality of its kind. Often, when an unexpected guest arrived, one would go to buy extra food from those shops where there are rows and rows of the roasted meats hanging in the window. They are now to be found in the Chinatown area of most western cities.

INDEX

Aubergines, stuffed 108
Bamboo leaves 112
   for wrapping food 32
Bamboo shoots 20, 21, 24, 32, 38, 84, 112
   stir-fried, with shredded chicken 66
Beans (green)
   stir-fried, with beef 64
   stir-fried, with pork 18
Bean sprouts
   in filling for Spring Rolls 48
Beef
   in filling for Spicy Rolls 68
   lemon beef soup 40
   stir-fried, with black soy beans 64, *65*
   stir-fried, with green peppers 50, *51*
Black soy beans 113
   with steamed grey mullet 92, *93*
   with stir-fried beef 50, 64, *65*
Braising 125
Bread (steamed wheat) 13
Broad beans
   stir-fried with chicken breast 72

Cabbage
   Chinese (see Chinese cabbage)
   in fillings 20, 68
   pickled 18, 66, 67, 118
Cakes 75
   author's own 74
   Moon Cake 8
Cantonese cuisine 11
   typical dishes 24, *25*, 30, 34, *35*, 48, *49*, 80, *81*,
     86, 92, *93*, 96, *97*
Celery
   stir-fried with shredded chicken 98, *99*
Chicken
   braised, with stir-fried leeks 96, *97*
   diced, stir-fried *73*
   diced, stir-fried, with bean paste and green
     peppers 46
   green and white chicken soup 100
   in deep-fried paper parcels 82
   quick-fried breasts with broad beans 72
   roast, stuffed ('beggar chicken') 20
   shredded, stir-fried with celery 98 *99*
   shredded, stir-fried with pickled cabbage 66, *67*
   steamed, whole, with sesame sauce 16
   stir-fried breasts in plum sauce 38, *39*
   stock 34
Chilli 12, 121
Chilli sauce (sweet) 56
China (food in)
   banquets 6
   breakfast 9

China (continued)
   desserts 6
   Dim Sum 10
   for festivals 7–8
   for New Year 8, 70
   main meal 7, 10
   mid-day meal 10
   regional cuisines 11–13
   restaurants 10
   supper 10
   vegetarian 8
Chinese cabbage 114
   stir-fried 31, *31*
   storing 12
   use of 113–4
   with meatballs 28, *29*
Chinese gooseberry 111
Chinese leaves
   see Chinese Cabbage
Choy Sum 11
Cilantro 114
Cinnamon 117
Cleaver 15, 21, *41*, 123
Cloves 117
Cod
   stir-fried, in stock 26
   in spinach parcel soup 102
Congee 9
Coriander 114
Cucumber
   with Peking Duck 54
Deep frying 14, 69, 125
Dicing *41*, 123
Dim Sum 10, 70
Duck
   in sausages 115
   roast 'Peking Duck' 54

Egg white
   in green and white chicken soup 100

Fennel (seed) 117
Figs (preserved) 71
Fire pot 103, *103*
Fish
   in spinach parcel soup 102
   intestines *85*, 116
   salted 9, *105*
   smoked over tea 104
   steamed 80 *81*, 92, *93*
   stir-fried, in stock 26
   stock 26
   stuffed fillets of 84
Five spice powder 30, 32, 68, 106, 115

Garlic 12, 17
Ginger 12, 17, 80
   and stir-fried prawns 90
   pickled, with Thousand Year Eggs 101

Halibut
   smoked over tea 104
Hoi Sin sauce 54, 118

Jung 7, 32, 33

Kiwi fruit 110, *111*
Kum Quat 71

Lamb 12
   stir-fried, with green peppers 78
Leek
   stir-fried, with braised chicken 96, *97*
Lemon
   lemon beef soup 40
   with steamed grey mullet 92, *93*
Lettuce 91
   used to hold food 38, *39*
Lin-Go 8, 70
Lotus leaf 20

Mangetout peas
   see Snow Peas
Marinade
   for Cantonese pork fillet 86
   for halibut 104
   for spare ribs 106
Meatballs 28, *29*
Melon
   bitter 113
   silk 11
Mincing 19, 124
Monkfish
   in spinach parcel soup 102
   stir-fried, in stock 26
Mullet (grey)
   steamed, with lemon 92, *93*
Mushrooms (Chinese dried) 32, 38, 48, 80, 84, *85*,
   114
   Silver Ears 120
Mutton 12

Noodles
   boiled 62, *63*
   fried, with beef and green peppers 50, *51*
   transparent, 89
   transparent, with dried shrimps 88
   yam noodles, with stir-fried pork 42, *43*

Olives (liquorice) 71

Pancakes 79
    for Peking Duck 54
    used to hold food with 55, 78
Paper parcels (deep fried) 10, 82, 83
Parsley (Chinese) 114
Pastry
    for author's own cake 74
    for Spring Onion Savoury 76
Peel (dried) 115
Peking cuisine 11, 12
    typical dishes 26, 36, *37*, 38, *39*, 54, 55, 88
Pepper (spice)
    lower peppercorns 117
    Szechuan 16, 106, *107*
Peppers (green) 45
    stir-fried, with beef and green peppers 50, *51*
    stir-fried, with chicken 46
    stir-fried, with lamb 78
Persimmon (dried) 71
Pineapple
    part of sweet and sour sauce 56
Plum sauce 38, *39*, 84, 118
Pomelo 111, *111*
Pork
    braised leg of 36, *37*
    in deep-fried paper parcels 82
    in filling for Spring Rolls 48
    in filling for Wun-Tun 34
    in stuffing for chicken 20
    meatballs, with Chinese cabbage 28, *29*
    spare ribs 106, *107*
    stir-fried, with green beans 18
    stir-fried, with mushrooms 24, *25*
    stir-fried, with yam noodles 42, *43*
Prawns 91
    in fried rice 52, *53*
    stir-fried, with ginger 90
    stir-fried, with spring onions 22, *23*
Preparation
    ahead of time 9
    importance of 6, 123
    methods of 123–126
Prunes 71

Quail
    marinated and tea-smoked 30

Red-stewing 126
Rice
    fried, with prawns 52, *53*
    plain boiled 27, *27*
Rice (glutinous) 117
    in Lin-Go 70
    steamed dumplings of 32

Rice flour (glutinous) 117
Rice wine 120
Roasting 126

Sak 120
Sand pot 14, 28, 37, 97
Saté sauce 119
Sausages (Chinese) 87 115
    with stir-fried snow peas 60 *61*
Scallops 95
    steamed 94
    stir-fried 44, *45*
Scoop 15
Scoring 124
Sea bass (steamed) 80
Seafood (abundance of) 11
Sesame
    oil 119
    sauce 16
    seeds 119
Shanghai cuisine 11, 12
    typical dishes 28, *29*, 66
Shaoshing wine 120
Shredding 21, 41, 123
Shrimps (dried) 116
    with transparent noodles 88
Sin Mai 126
Slicing 21 41 123
Smoking 126
    halibut 104
    quail 30
Snow Peas 120
    stir-fried, with Chinese sausages 60, *61*
Sole
    fillet stuffed with vegetables 84
Soup
    as accompaniment 10
    green and white chicken soup 100
    lemon beef 40
    served in a fire pot *103*
    spinach parcel soup 102
    Wun-Tun, with watercress 34, *35*
Soy Beans
    in yellow bean sauce 122
    see also Black soy beans
Soy sauce (kinds of) 112
Spare ribs 106, *107*
Spatula 15
Spicy rolls 68, *69*
Spinach
    in green and white chicken soup 100
    spinach parcel soup 102
Spring onion 51, 54
    'flowers' (decoration) 30

Spring onion (continued)
    savory 76
    with Peking Duck 54
    with steamed scallops 94
Spring roll paper 48, 49 68
Spring rolls 48, 49, 68
Spring rolls 48, 49, 69
Star anise 30, 104, 106, *107*, 117, 121
Steaming 14, 125
Steaming baskets
    for serving 10
    use of 14, 125
Steaming rack 14, 125
Stir frying 73, 124
Strainer 15
Sugar (Chinese) 8, 115
    in Lin-Go 70
    with Snow Ears 110
Sweet and sour sauce 56
Szechuan cuisine 11, 12
    typical dishes 18
Szechuan paste 121

Tea (for smoking food) 30, 104, 126
Thousand year eggs 101, *101*
Toffee apples 58, *59*
Toffee bananas 58, *59*
Trout (steamed) 80, *81*
Turbot
    stir-fried, in stock 26
    in spinach parcel soup 102

Un Sin Poy 12

Water chestnuts 28, 122
Watercress
    in soup, with Wun-Tun 34, *35*
Wok
    use of 13
    for steaming 14, 125
Wok ring 14
Wok stirrer 15
Wooden Ears (mushroons) 121
    stir fried, with sliced pork 24, *25*
Wun Tin Mein
    see Paper parcels
Wun-Tun 34, 77
    skins, method of making, 34
    in soup, with watercress 34, *35*
    fried, with sweet and sour sauce 56, *57*

Yam noodles
    with stir-fried pork 42, *43*
Yellow bean sauce
    with stir-fried chicken 46